PREMIERSHIP WINNERS

First published in Great Britain in 1998 by
Dempsey Parr
13 Whiteladies Road
Clifton
Bristol BS8 1PB

ISBN: 1-84084-208-3

Produced for Dempsey Parr by Prima Creative Services

Editorial director Roger Kean
Managing editor Steve Faragher (Content E.D.B.)

Design and repro by Prima Creative Services
Additional design by Maryanne Booth

Printed and bound in Italy

Acknowledgements
The publisher would like to thank Tim Smith (Content E.D>B) , Nick Moyle and Stuart Weir for their invaluable help in the production of this book.

Picture Acknowledgements
The publisher would like to thank Allsport, Action Images and Photo News Scotland for their help and the kind permission to reproduce the photographs used in this book.

Contents

 4 RETROSPECTIVE
Thrills and spills – it's been a year to remember

 6 THE SCOTTISH PREMIER LEAGUE CLUBS
A brief insight into how the teams stacked up

8 ABERDEEN
It's been an interesting season for the Dons

12 CELTIC
The Bhoys believed the barren years were over

 16 DUNDEE UNITED
The Terrors found it hard to frighten anyone

20 DUNFERMLINE ATHLETIC
Is this the formula to keep Dunfermline up?

24 HEART OF MIDLOTHIAN
Hearts helped raise expectations for a while

 28 HIBERNIAN
It started stunningly, then went horribly wrong

32 KILMARNOCK
Killie promised better things for the future

36 MOTHERWELL
A year Well supporters will want to forget

 40 RANGERS
The Gers stumbled from drama to crisis and back

44 ST JOHNSTONE
The Saints had more than their fair share of glory

 **48** OTHER COMPETITIONS
A round-up of Championship events

 60 MONTH-BY-MONTH
The statistics for every game of the season

66 AUGUST 1997
Rangers' tenth successive title looks possible...

 68 SEPTEMBER 1997
Good performances put Edinburgh teams in front

 70 OCTOBER 1997
Three teams take turns at the top

 72 NOVEMBER 1997
The Edinburgh and Glasgow derbies dominate

 74 DECEMBER 1997
The Old Firm closes in, but Hearts won't lie down

 76 JANUARY 1998
No clarity – the top three are neck and neck

 78 FEBRUARY 1998
In this race, three's a crowd

 80 MARCH 1998
The title's still wide open – Rangers or Celtic?

 82 APRIL 1998
Celtic defeat Kilmarnock to go three points ahead

 84 LAST GAMES OF THE SEASON
Up-to-the-minute spellbinding action

 92 END OF SEASON STATISTICS
Everything you need to know about 1997/98

 93 A CELTIC CELEBRATION
The pictures say it all...

Introduction

the auld firm plus one

Perched on the edge of history, Rangers assembled a mighty host to ensure a ten-in-a-row footballing victory. Standing between them and destiny were a team of Bhoys with valiant Hearts.

W ould they do it? Or could they be stopped? Could the mighty Glasgow Rangers who had matched Celtic's unprecedented record of nine league championships in a row, go one better and make it ten? In the polarised world of Scottish football, the only team anyone expected to be able to stop the Rangers colossus from achieving their aim was Celtic. Yet Celtic were starting the season with a new coach and two of their most influential players at loggerheads with the club. It looked highly unlikely.

Dundee United were potential champions too. Their run of 13 straight victories in the latter part of the previous season, beating Rangers and Celtic on the way, was record enough to warn the rest of the league of their potential. But the squad was ageing and, as the season closed, teams were coping with United's threat.

No one fancied Hearts. Almost imperceptibly though, Jim Jefferies had shaped and crafted a side that blended youth with experience and skill with graft. What's more, their attacking formations and attractive style of play could be a thing of beauty to watch in full flow.

And then there was the Rangers' challenge itself. The £15 million pre-season strengthening of the squad by Walter Smith must have struck fear into the hearts of even the most stalwart managers. A brace of unlucky injuries robbed the Gers of the use of many of these signings, but the sheer depth of the Rangers' squad ensured that they weren't missed too much. Marco Negri, a sultry and mostly unknown Italian striker made an immediate and devastating impact on the league. His goal tally of 30 goals by December put him on target to smash the previous Rangers record of 49 goals in one season held by Ali McCoist.

But Rangers then started showing cracks in their defence which had never been seen before. It was this occasional stuttering which let Hearts and Celtic constantly overtake and swap places with each other and the Gers. It made for a highly-charged, exciting and vibrant league campaign – everything seemed to have come to the good just as the league was going to be changed.

The more the media, pundits and fans wrote off the credible Hearts' challenge, the more Hearts rose to the occasion to prove their doubters wrong. Only in their meetings with Auld Firm did their resolve falter. Compensating for this, they were more consistent in their meetings with other Premier teams than either Auld Firm team. Eventually, in April, Hearts finally faltered, but they'll be back.

The main stage, almost inevitably was left to the Auld Firm to play out.

How the Scottish Premier finished in 1996–97

Rangers	36	80
Celtic	36	75
Dundee United	36	60
Hearts	36	52
Dunfermline	36	45
Aberdeen	36	44
Kilmarnock	36	39
Motherwell	36	38
Hibernian	36	38
Raith Rovers	36	25

Scottish Division One 1996–97

St Johnstone promoted	36	80
Airdrieonians	36	60
Dundee	36	58
St Mirren	36	58
Falkirk	36	54
Partick Thistle	36	48

Allsport

Welcome to the fight
1997-1998

Whichever way you cut it, this was always going to be an historic season. But with Glasgow awaiting the breaking of an unbreakable record, Edinburgh decided to put in a bid for the Premiership...

Ten-in-a-row was the statistic that obsessed everyone it seemed. However, with Rangers and Celtic in a fight to the death, it was Jim Jeffries' Hearts who really stirred up the mix. So a breathless finish was on the cards...

ABERDEEN > > > > > > > > > > > 8

A dismal start to the season, a change in managers and a promising future. It's been an interesting season for the Dons.

CELTIC > > > > > > > > > > > > 12

Despite losing a manager and three high-profile stars, Celtic still managed to retain a belief that this season might just end their barren years.

DUNDEE UNITED > > > > > > > > 16

The Terrors were finding it hard to frighten anyone this season, especially in the beginning...

for the Premiership

DUNFERMLINE ATHLETIC > > > **20**

The second season since Dunfermline won promotion and they look like they've discovered the formula that'll let them stay up.

HEART OF MIDLOTHIAN > > > > **24**

In a championship suffering the monotony with which Rangers won it, Jim Jefferies' Hearts helped raise the exchange rate for an extended period.

HIBERNIAN > > > > > > > > > **28**

Hibs confounded their critics by climbing to and holding the league lead for almost two months. Then it all went horribly wrong...

KILMARNOCK > > > > > > > > > **32**

Having finished the previous season as Scottish Cup winners and with a fine run of league form, Kilmarnock promised better things for the future.

MOTHERWELL > > > > > > > > > **36**

Lacklustre performances and a dispirited atmosphere led to a horrific season which Well's supporters will remember for all the wrong reasons

RANGERS > > > > > > > > > > **40**

Rangers stumbled from drama to crisis. Marco Negri's skills kept them in the race, but when his talent failed him the team did not know what to do.

ST JOHNSTONE > > > > > > > > **44**

The Saints had their fair share of glory with their victory over Rangers which rubber-stamped their Premier credentials for the new millennium.

Aberdeen

the dons

A dismal start to the season, a change in managers and a promising future. It's been an interesting season for the Dons.

This season saw Aberdeen achieve the worst league start in their 94 year club history. In their first eight games they failed to record one victory, gaining only three points from three draws. It brought the dismal statistic that, for the year, Aberdeen had only won two games in 27 starts. The team, like the manager, were rock bottom and bereft of ideas.

Speculation about Roy Aitken's future was continually staved off by vice-chairman Stuart Milne: "Dismissing Roy has never been on the agenda. One of the sad things in football is that managerial change is seen as the only solution."

But despite the noises, managerial change was not only needed, it was on the cards. The only light in an otherwise very dark tunnel was provided by a Coca-Cola Cup run which took the Dons all the way to the semi-finals, where they faced Dundee United at Tynecastle. The Terrors were the first Premier opposition Aberdeen had to face in the competition and it was perhaps no coincidence that their run stopped there.

A small respite was achieved when the team recorded consecutive victories over fellow relegation strugglers Hibernian and Motherwell. The final nail in the coffin though was hammered in by the Tangerine Terrors at Tannadice. Live on television, Aberdeen were routed with clinical efficiency. If it hadn't been for a heroic performance from Scotland's veteran goalkeeper Jim Leighton, the final score of 5-0 could have been even more embarrassing.

"He's on the dole, he's on the dole, Aitken's on the dole" sang the gleefully unsympathetic home crowd. And they were right. By Monday Aitken was out of a job.

The Pittodrie fans were hardly ecstatic at the announcement of Alex Miller as the new manager. He had a reputation for being boring, but he also turned around the Dons' defensive record. In the new year, it took the visit of Celtic at the end of March before 'fortress Pittodrie' was breached with a goal.

Coupled with a rejuvenated Eoin Jess and a new belief circulating round the team, next season should bring better things for the Dons.

CLUB FACTS

Stadium: **Pittodrie Stadium**
01224 632328
Capacity: **21,634**
Managers: **Roy Aitken, Alex Miller**
Club Captain: **Jim Leighton**
League Position in last five years:
1992-93 2nd
1993-94 2nd
1994-95 9th
1995-96 3rd
1996-97 6th

TRANSFERS IN

Date	Player	From	Fee
6/97	Eoin Jess	Coventry City	£700k
6/97	James Leighton	Hibernian	£1m
6/97	Brian O'Neil	Celtic	£750k
6/97	Gary Smith	Stade Rennais	£200k
8/97	Lee Barclay	Lewis United	nominal
8/97	Christopher Clark	Hermes	nominal
8/97	Richard Gillies	St. Mirren	£250k
8/97	Michael Hart	Stoneywood	nominal
8/97	Kevin Milne	Hermes	nominal
7/97	Michael Newell	Birmingham City	400-700k
8/97	Karl Williamson	Ellon United	nominal

TRANSFERS OUT

No players sold this season

Date	Player	To	Fee
1/98	Derek Whyte	Middlesbrough	not disclosed

GAME OF THE SEASON

15 November 1997
Aberdeen (1) 1 Jess 45
Rangers (0) 1 Albertz 75
Bookings: Anderson, O'Neil, Glass, Smith (Aberdeen)
Cleland, McCall (Rangers)
Attendance: 18,205 Referee: K Clark (Paisley)

Caretaker manager Keith Burkinshaw put Eoin Jess into his favoured position just behind the strikers. It worked a treat. Against the run of play, Jess gives Aberdeen the lead with a 20-yard volley. The fight in Aberdeen's play which was previously absent comes to the fore. Jess finally shoulders the responsibility expected of him.

Brian O'Neil works hard for the ball against Robbie Winters, but the Dons were hammered 5–0 by Dundee on the 5th November.

Photo News Scotland

Eoin Jess

a question of confidence

Over rated, over paid, and over here might still appear in the obituary columns for Aberdeen and Scotland's most enigmatic footballing son, Eoin Jess.

In the harsh world of footballing economics, nothing paints a starker picture of form and talent than the £1.7 million Coventry City paid Aberdeen for Eoin Jess in February 1996 and the £650,000 the Dons bought him back for in July 1997. Roy Aitken, the then Aberdeen manager, made the decision to save a career sinking fast because he wanted Jess "to make the whole team tick." It didn't happen. Jess put it down to a lack of confidence and a team that weren't playing solidly enough: "I'm just a player who thrives on confidence. If I could find a consistent confidence I'd be a consistent player."

Despite the confidence shown in him by Aitken, he was unable to produce the goods. That was until, on the eve of Alex Miller's appearance at Pittodrie, he hit Rangers with a beautifully executed goal which reminded Dons' fans of performances of yesteryear. "I am the sort of player whose whole season can be transformed by one touch," he said afterwards.

As the rest of the season proved, goalscoring was only a fraction of the 'one touch' which he seemed to gain so much confidence from. When on song he proved that he is still one of the most imaginative and skillful players in the country. His second half performance against Hibs in their 2–2 league draw evoked the following praise from Miller: "No offence to any other player but Jess was head and shoulders above the rest". Incisive passes from his twinkle toes cut open defences with the precision of a surgeon's scalpel. When the space wasn't there, his skill and imagination helped him create it – as if by magic. In conjunction with the ever clinical Billy Dodds and the energetic Dean Windass, Jess helped Aberdeen lift themselves out of the relegation dogfight.

His resurgence in form must have seemed like an ironic blow to the sacked Aitken. Miller, his successor as manager, had been one of the main proponents behind the decision to get rid of Jess from Coventry City when he was assistant manager there. And yet Miller is also the chief suspect behind the effusive praise heaped on Jess by Craig Brown and his consequent Scotland call up in the friendly against Denmark.

Brown felt that an on form Jess would be the perfect foil for a striking partnership with Kevin Gallacher. That Brown is prepared to show so much confidence in a player described by Gordon Strachan as possessing "an X factor" is either foolhardy or laudable.

Scotland fans may not be so effusive with their praise or their confidence. The ball, as they say, is in Jess's half.

Eoin Jess Statistics

Born: 13th December 1970

Height: 5ft 9.5

Weight: 11st 6lbs

Previous Clubs:
 1987–95 Aberdeen
 1995–97 Coventry City
 1997–98 Aberdeen

Celtic

the bhoys

Despite winning nothing the previous season, and losing a manager and three high profile stars, Celtic still managed to retain a belief that this season might just end their barren years.

Out with the old and in with the new summed up the start to the new championship challenge launched by the Premier League's proverbial Glasgow losers, Celtic.

In came Wim Jansen a continental coach with a set of new ideas and a new style concentrated more on solidity in defence and muscle and creativity in midfield. Whinges that this resulted in a sterile method of play were mostly true, but the results on the field and the mounting number of clean sheets recorded by the defence achieved title-worthy points if nothing else. One element missing from transforming Celtic into a formidable unit was the inclusion of a merciless striker in the mould of a Marco Negri or Jorge Cadete.

The acquisition of Harald Brattbakk from Norwegian champions Rosenborg for £2 million was supposed to fill the blank, but somewhere along the line the striker, who looked like a building society manager, managed to play like one as well. Despite making his debut in December, Brattbakk only managed to score in a paltry two league games throughout the rest of the campaign.

Celtic had to rely on goals coming from everywhere else in the field. Craig Burley relished the extra freedom allowed him in his midfield role and notched up a creditable tally of goals out-achieving many other teams' main strikers. Henrik Larsson, despite playing best in the role of goal provider, also achieved an outstanding goal record and finished as Celtic's top scorer.

Despite playing some fine flowing football, Celtic too often managed to suffer from lapses of concentration that cost them needless points. Their total domination of Hearts in the two teams' third meeting of the season in February was a case in point. In their opponents' half and with only seconds left to go to full time, Celtic managed to be dispossessed and lost a needless goal.

Performances like these managed to keep Rangers in touch with the title. Celtic lacked the killer efficiency that had worked for the Gers in the past nine seasons. In the end, though, the Bhoys didn't so much win the championship as Rangers threw it away.

Yet, even then Celtic stuttered. When Kilmarnock provided the shock of the season by inflicting the only Ibrox defeat of Rangers in the second last match of the season, the Bhoys couldn't wrap up the title the next day against Dunfermline. They ran out of steam and settled for an insipid draw. That it took to the last match for the championship to be decided was farcical for everyone concerned.

GAME OF THE SEASON
2 January 1998
Celtic 2 (0) Burley 66, Lambert 85
Rangers 0 (0)
Bookings: Lambert, Boyd. McCall, Negri, Gough
Attendance: 49350 Referee: H Dallas (Motherwell)

Celtic recorded their first league win over Rangers in 11 games and the first in the New Year match since 1988 – their centenary season and the last time they won a championship. Enrico Annoni's shackling of Laudrup and the late appearance of Gascoigne contributed to an ascendancy from Celtic from which Rangers never recovered. The die appeared to have been cast in favour of the Bhoys.

CLUB FACTS
Stadium: Celtic Park
0141 556 2611
Capacity: 50,550
Manager: **Wim Jansen**
Club Captain: **Tom Boyd**
League Position in last five years:
1992/93: 3rd
1993/94: 4th
1994/95: 4th
1995/96: 2nd
1996/97: 2nd

TRANSFERS IN			
6/97	Craig Burley	Chelsea	£2.5m
6/97	Darren Jackson	Hibernian	£1m
6/97	Henrik Larsson	Feyenoord	£650k
6/97	Stephane Mahe	Stade Rennais	£450k
8/97	Regi Blinker	Sheffield Wed	£1.5m
8/97	Jonathon Gould	Bradford City	nominal
9/97	Marc Rieper	West Ham United	£1.4m
11/97	Paul Lambert	Borussia Dortmund	£1.7m
12/97	Harald Brattbakk	Rosenborg	£2m

TRANSFERS OUT			
8/97	Chris Hay	Swindon	£330k
8/97	Peter Grant	Norwich	£200k
8/97	Paddy Kelly	Newcastle	Free
9/97	Paolo Di Canio	Sheffield Wed	£3m
3/98	Stuart Gray	Reading	£100k

Enrico Annoni has the reach over Brian Laudrup, as the Bhoys take rival Rangers 2–0 on 2nd January.

Henrik Larsson

not dreadlocked

A lesser man would have been daunted by the task of pleasing Celtic supporters in the wake of Cadete or di Canio, but Henrik Larsson's supreme confidence won goals and friends.

Winning the heart of the demanding and passionate crowd who follow Glasgow Celtic was never going to be easy for Henrik Larsson. Following in the wake of clinical goalscoring machine Jorge Cadete and the ever flamboyant Paulo di Canio could have made a lesser player baulk at the height of expectation facing them.

But not for this dreadlock-sporting hairband-wearing Swede. Supreme confidence in his ability and a burning desire to prove himself as the mainstay of a team eventually saw him heading in Scotland's direction. A clause written into his Feyenoord contract that he could leave if an offer of £650,000 was made for him, combined with the desire of new Celtic coach Wim Jansen to add him to the team, saw the two meet up once again at the same club.

Jansen had been chiefly responsible for Larsson's transfer to Feyenoord in 1993. The £650,000 spent turned out to be the best foreign buy per overall performance that the Scottish league has seen for many seasons. As a measure of the player, his league tally of goals is testimony enough. But such a measure belies the depth of the rest of Larsson's game.

Holding off defenders while linking with the rest of the team has helped produce goals from all manner of

Celtic's players. His greatest asset, however, lies in his ability to take a pass and move into space without hindering or altering the course of the ball. Such ability has left many a midfield and defensive player looking stupid.

It is still open to speculation what kind of goal record Celtic could have achieved if they had managed to procure an out-and-out striker with the clinical finishing of a Cadete or a Van Hoodjidonk. In the four-goal dissolution of Kilmarnock in February, Harald Brattbakk, the mostly-failed striker from Rosenborg, took the match accolade for all four goals that he scored. But the performance was only made possible due to the incisive passing and quick thinking of Larsson. Without his contribution, Kilmarnock might have had a chance and Brattbakk would have been less noticeable.

The fluidity of Larsson's movement coupled with the depth from which he can make goal endangering runs means that his threat can never be discounted. It's still somewhat of a mystery why he was axed from Sweden's international side. When asked if he thought it might be due to playing in a lesser league and that he wasn't good enough he replied; "I can't accept that idea. Here, the game is faster, and

Henrik Larsson statistics

Born: 20th September 1971

Height: 5ft 10in

Weight: 11st 11lbs

Previous Clubs:
1989–93 Helsingborgs
1993–97 Feyenoord
1997— Glasgow Celtic

when it is faster you need a lot more technique."

Dundee United

the terrors

The Terrors were finding it hard to frighten anyone this season, especially in the beginning...

Last season, after a bumpy first quarter, Dundee United put on a power performance which would have seen them as creditable title challengers had it not been for their poor start. They finished third in the league and were unlucky to be put out of the semi-final of the Scottish Cup. Unsurprisingly, the expectations of the fans were raised for the new season. Those expectations were cruelly dashed though when, after the first two months of play, United failed to produce one victory. Their first victory eventually arrived against Motherwell with an emphatic 4–0 drubbing – with The Terrors finally displaying the pacy counter-attacking style the fans and manager knew they were capable of.

That victory kick-started a glorious run of five straight victories and United again believed that any team in the league was there for the taking. This belief was cruelly dashed by Celtic in a league clash a week before the two teams were due to meet in the final of the Coca-Cola Cup. United's discipline deserted them and Celtic reaped the reward by sticking four goals past a very shaky Sieb Dykstra.

The result seemed to undermine United's confidence to the core and in the Cup Final the next week, they lay down to a very beatable Celtic side.

Still worse was to happen. Their goal-making machinery dried up and they failed to score in four consecutive matches. Rumbles of discontent with the manager began to reverberate around Tannadice. Not so much because of the results, but more because of the dullness and apathy afflicting the team. Not even the introduction in January of the impressive Cameroon international Jean Jacque Misse-Misse could save United from blandness.

Another meeting with Celtic in the quarter-final of the Scottish Cup produced one of the best games of the season. But it was to no avail. A cruel own goal by Erik Pedersen in injury time put paid to any European aspirations held by United.

Sadly, it all ended in a mild flirtation with the relegation dogfight at the bottom, which doesn't bode well for next season.

CLUB FACTS

Stadium: **Tannadice Park**
  01382 833166
Capacity: **12,616**
Manager: **Tommy MacLean**
Club Captain: **David Bowman**
League Position in last five years:
1992-93 4th
1993-94 6th
1994-95 10th
1995-96 2nd (1st Division)
1996-97 3rd

TRANSFERS IN

9/97	Joseph Bryers	Lanark United	nominal
7/97	Gareth Dailly	Lochee United	nominal
9/97	Christopher Devine	Lanark United	nominal
8/97	Goran Marklund	Vaslund Idrottsforening	£125k
1/98	Jean J Misse-Misse	Trabzonspor	monthly

TRANSFERS OUT

11/97	Ian Johnson	Huddersfield	£90k
3/98	Jean J Misse-Misse	Chesterfield	NC

GAME OF THE SEASON

9th November 1997
Dundee United (3) 5 Olofsson 17; 83, Zetterlund 18
McLaren 21, Easton 87
Aberdeen (0) 0
Bookings: Windass (Sent Off)
Attendance: 7,893 Referee: Stuart Dougal

Dean Windass is sent off, Kjell Olofsson runs rampant, Jim Leighton produces one of his finest performances of the season, Roy Aitken is sacked, and live television captures all the drama and excitement. Aberdeen thought they had turned the corner with their previous back to back victories. This result brought them down to earth with a bang.

Rowson can't keep his hands off Eric Pederson as Dundee terrorises Aberdeen 5–0 on 9th November.

Steven Pressley

heartbreaker

There's a great tradition of Scottish players going down south and returning better players than before. Steven Pressley's no exception...

The decision by Steven 'Elvis' Pressley to leave Rangers in 1994 for Coventry City proved to be an inspirational choice. Having established himself as a formidable central defender, Dundee United brought him back to Scotland for a club record signing fee of £750,000. His pivotal role alongside the wily intelligence and guile of Maurice Malpas lead to a defensive partnership likened to the cast of 'Heartbreak High' because of its ability to frustrate attackers. He was instrumental in the immediate bounceback of United from the First Division to their rightful home in the Premier.

Recognising his immaculate aggression and physical robustness, Tommy MacLean drummed into Pressley's head that he wanted him to be the key to United's devastating counter attacks.

The faith shown in the player was rewarded when, last season, United went on a record breaking unbeaten run in the Premier to finish third and claim a UEFA place in Europe.

This season, despite mostly solid performances from Pressley, United have stuttered. Many claim that their counter attacking style had been 'found out'. Most telling for United was their performance against Celtic. Having met

an unprecedented six times, once in the final of the Coca-Cola Cup, once in the Scottish Cup and four times in the league, United lost five times, narrowly avoiding being whitewashed in the last league match between the two.

MacLean hinted before the Coca-Cola final that he was less than impressed with Pressley's performance against Henrik Larsson. The Swede proved too quick in the thinking department and too quick on the field of play for Pressley to contain him in the manner the defender had contained so many other goalscoring threats.

Despite that, there's no doubting that Pressley has been a heartbreaker to the numerous other teams facing United. He himself cites Maurice Malpas as a major factor in his improvement in the game; "He's been a massive influence on me. I like to think that I've learned so much from him."

He certainly learned enough to be selected for the Scotland B international against Wales. Unfortunately, a niggling foot injury picked up during the Scottish Cup quarter final against Celtic scuppered the opportunity. There's no doubt there will be more opportunities in the future. He captained the Under-21 Scotland squad. He's still only 24 and the partnership with Malpas should

Steven Pressley statistics

Born: 11th Oct 73

Height: 6ft

Weight: 11st

Previous Clubs:
  1990–94 Rangers
  1994–95 Coventry City
  1995— Dundee United

produce more learning from the willing student.

Due to the Bosman ruling, he may not be with United at the end of the season. Tommy MacLean should prove too shrewd a manager to let such a potential disaster happen.

Dunfermline Athletic

the pars

The second season since Dunfermline won promotion and they look like they've discovered the formula that'll let them stay up.

The archetypal yo-yo club, Dunfermline's record over the past ten years highlights and endorses the argument that the Scottish Premier League should be expanded to make way for at least another two entrants. St Johnstone may have been the bookies' favourites for the drop, but Dunfermline were the team the pundits and supporters most expected to go down. Their robust, resilient, non-stop harrying style of play earned them an unfair reputation as a route one team bereft of ideas. That they used height to their advantage was beyond question, but when tactics dictated Dunfermline surprised the opposition with an incisiveness on the deck that belied expectations.

A sprightly start to the season saw them take full points from Hearts and Celtic in consecutive weeks. However,

any high flying ideas were quickly dispelled after a 5–2 drubbing from Hibernian at Easter Road. A drop in their normally ebullient endeavours witnessed a 7–0 thrashing at Ibrox which signalled a complete reversal in fortune, punctuated only by a couple of straight victories over St Johnstone and Hibernian. Alarm bells started ringing from the end of November to the end of January when, after an unlucky defeat at Kilmarnock, they failed to record a victory in their next seven matches. This brought their tally to nine games without a win. Things got so bad that they failed to score a goal in over 540 minutes of league football. Home attendances began to dwindle significantly as freefall toward the relegation zone beckoned.

On the last day of January the visit of Kilmarnock bore all the hallmarks of

yet another loss. Killie had recorded eight games without defeat. When the visitors scored in the opening five minutes the home support braced themselves for the worst. But it never happened. Drawing on their psychological reserves Dunfermline fought back spiritedly to record their highest victory of the season, 3–2. From then on in, they ensured their Premier League safety.

CLUB FACTS
Stadium: **East End Park**
01383 724295
Capacity: **12,968**
Manager: **Bert Paton**
Team Captain: **Craig Robertson**
League Position in last five years:
1992-93 3rd (1st Div)
1993-94 2nd (1st Div)
1994-95 2nd (1st Div)
1995-96 1st (1st Div)
1996-97 5th

TRANSFERS IN			
7/97	David Barnett	Birmingham City	monthly
9/97	Simon Kaldjob	Stade Brest	monthly
6/97	Greg Shields	Rangers	£175k
11/97	Sergio Duarte	Boavista Porto	free
10/97	George Shaw	Dundee	nominal

TRANSFERS OUT			
4/98	David Barnett	Port Vale	free

GAME OF THE SEASON
31 January 1998
Dunfermline (1) 3 Barnett 41, Smith 67, Shaw 76
Kilmarnock (1) 2 Vareille 2, Roberts 85
Bookings: Shaw, Smith, Sharp, Bingham (Dundee)
Baker (Kilmarnock)
Attendance: 4,903 Referee: K Clark (Paisley)

When the league's form team met the league's out of form team, everyone expected the inevitable. Dunfermline however had not read the script. Ignoring the form book, they rolled up their sleeves and got stuck into Killie with gusto. Two sucker punches in the second half clinched the result and sent the Ayrshiremen home to lick their wounds.

Dunfermline got off to a good start, cracking 2–1 against Celtic in August. Alan Moore and Celtic's David Hannah fight it out for possession.

Action Images

Andrew Smith

andy capped?

If ever a player could be described as reflecting the character of a club, Dunfermline Athletic's awkward, fans' favourite, beanpole striker Andy Smith is him.

Weighing in at a bustling 175 pounds, Andy Smith's six-foot-plus frame and physically robust style of play is used to devastating effect on opposition defences. Strong in the air, handy on the ground, Smith makes up for what he lacks in skill with an incredible work rate. After Smith roasted Motherwell's on-loan defender Rob Newman in the two team's March encounter at East End Park, the battered defender felt prompted to praise him: "He is one of the most difficult opponents in the league – he never gives you a moment's peace on the ball."

Newman's comments helped reinforce the growing clamour that Smith should at least have been selected for a place in the pre-World Cup Scottish B internationals: "If he was called into the international squad he would improve as a player," was Newman's opinion. It took all season, but eventually he got his chance by being included in the B squad for the match against the Norway Under-23 side at Tynecastle. Smith's phenomenal strike rate for the season was second only to that of Rangers' Marco Negri, making Smith the highest scoring native born player in the Division. As far as Dunfermline's fans were concerned, the quantity proved the quality. And who was to say that they were wrong?

Signed from arch-rivals Airdrieonians in July 1995, Bert Paton admitted that news of the transfer initially received a hostile greeting from Pars fans. "Andy was the enemy and the supporters used to ask me why I had signed that big B. They were ready to hang me from the stand for doing it, but now they'd lynch me from the rafters if I tried to sell him."

As befitting of the big man's good nature, he modestly played down the World Cup squad claims made on his behalf by reckoning he'd be following "200 strikers ahead of me".

The only bogey that Smith recognises is that against Celtic, who he failed to penetrate this season. He also failed to score against either Celtic last season. The Bhoys are too aware of his potential threat and Dunfermline's frailties to allow either to seriously threaten their footballing supremacy.

Despite that setback, his continual harrying of defences and desire to play the game knows no bounds. Opponents often comment that he never gives up and chases and makes chances out of situations others would have given up as lost.

This partly explains why this season was his most prolific in the goalscoring department ever. Dunfermline owe their Premier survival to Smith's spirit and never-say-die attitude. Who can say what might happen for the Pars when the strike partnership between Andy and the long term injured but now recovered Gerry Britton gets another chance to flourish?

Andrew Smith Statistics

Born: 27th November 1968

Height: 6'1"

Weight: 12st 7lbs

Previous Clubs:
  1990–95 Airdrieonians
  1995—   Dunfermline Athletic

Heart of Midlothian

the jambos

In a championship bearing the hallmark of devalued currency due to the monotony with which Rangers won it, Jim Jefferies' Hearts helped raise the exchange rate for an extended period.

This season, Hearts came as close to the Scottish version of Total Football as is ever likely to be seen at Tynecastle. Most encouraging for Hearts fans and the country as a whole was that it was based on a home-grown and youthful Scottish foundation. Things look rosy for the future. Despite failing a furlong from the winning post, the age of the team means that there must be more of the same to come.

Picking the quality that most stood out throughout the season is highly debatable due to the many qualities possessed by the side. Switchable and blistering pace supplied by Steve Fulton, Neil McCann, Colin Cameron and Jim Hamilton caught so many teams on the hop that by the time they started back pedalling to attempt recovery it was too late, the damage had been done. Composure came from the level head of Davie Weir, Stephane Adam and

youngest member of the team, Gary Naysmith. But these were only two qualities among many that helped sustain the team throughout the numerous exciting and highly charged matches thrown at them by the last Scottish Premier league.

As if to signal their intent in the title chase, Hearts soundly beat Aberdeen 4–1 at Tynecastle in the second week of August. It was their first home victory against the Dons since October 1994 and was also notable in that it was their highest Premier victory against that team.

Their fighting spirit and never-say-die attitude was sorely tested when, outgunned and outplayed by a rampant Celtic at Tynecastle, the team doggedly hung on and managed to snatch an undeserved injury time draw to stop the Glasgow team from going clear at the top of the table.

This resilience was called upon again the following week against the unpredictable Motherwell. Finding themselves 2–0 down on the verge of half time they managed to claw a goal back before the interval. The second half hung in the balance until, drawing on their resources they turned the game around and ended up cantering toward a 4–2 victory.

That they failed to defeat the Old Firm in any match proved to be their undoing. The last roll of the dice at home against Rangers in April finally crushed their championship dream underfoot. If however Jim Jefferies can further strengthen an already strong side, the Old Firm might finally face an east coast challenge able to break their tedious stranglehold on the Scottish scene.

GAME OF THE SEASON

8th February 1998
Hearts 1 (0) Quitongo 89
Celtic 1 (1) McNamara 14
Booked: Ritchie, Annoni, Burley, Lambert
Attendance: 17,657 **Referee:** B. Tait

Hearts show bottle. One of the claims that followed Hearts throughout their campaign was that they capitulated too easily when matched against the Old Firm. This match firmly dispelled that myth. Despite Celtic being in the ascendancy, holding a lead and playing out the match, Hearts never give up. They manage to steal a point on the verge of full time.

CLUB FACTS

Stadium: **Tynecastle**
  (0131) 200 7200
Capacity: **18,000**
Manager: **Jim Jefferies**
Club Captain: **Gary Locke**
League Position in last five years:
1992/93: 5th
1993/94: 7th
1994/95: 6th
1995/96: 4th
1996/97: 4th

TRANSFERS IN

6/97	Stephane Adam	Metz	Free
6/97	Thomas Flogel	Austria Vienna	Free
8/97	Craig Findlay	Whitburn Athletic	Nominal
10/97	Jose Quitongo	Hamilton Academical	£80k

TRANSFERS OUT

298	Pasquale Bruno	Wigan	No contract
1/98	Stephen Frail	Tranmere	£90k

Colin Cameron's blistering pace catches Ian Ferguson on the hop, but doesn't stop Rangers getting a 5–2 victory over Heart in December.

Neil McCann

no poor man's ryan giggs

With a career at international level already under his belt, Neil McCann seems to have done it all already, and he's only 24 years old.

In the body electric that was Heart of Midlothian this season, Steve Fulton provided the heart, Stefano Salvatori the muscle, Stephane Adam the brain, and Neil McCann the inspiration.

Without McCann's contribution, Hearts would not have made such a decisive impact on the psyche of Scottish football. His imaginative and insightful runs provided most of the supply for the numerous and outstanding goals scored by the Gorgie Road boys.

McCann himself puts the inspiration down to the day when, as a teenager with Dundee, he nutmegged ex-Rangers and Scotland legend Davie Cooper; "he slapped me on the bum, called me kid and said I had just done something brilliant...there and then I really began to think I could make it in this game."

And make it he did. His natural talent earned him 12 Scotland Under-21 call ups starting from April 1994. His goal in the semi of the 1996 Coca-Cola Cup catapulted First Division Dundee into the final and opened up the dream of Europe for the city of discovery. Aberdeen spoiled the dream, but they couldn't stop the onward march of the inspired McCann.

Jim Jefferies, one of the shrewdest and canny managers in the game scooped the winger up for a mere £250,000, gazumping Sturm Graz of Austria andCannes of France.

The investment was paid back with personal equity interest. In the same season that he joined Hearts he helped steer his side toward a Coca-Cola Cup final. This time Rangers stalled the dream, but kickstarted an enthralling final and a push for a European spot which was narrowly denied by a fourth place league finish.

This season, the title chasing aspirations of Hearts owed much to the movement, invention and free reign of McCann's imaginative play. That the chase failed so close to the winning post was neither the fault nor the intention of the inspired winger.

Craig Brown himself described McCann as "the poor man's Ryan Giggs". Despite the back page tabloid hoopla over the misinterpreted compliment, McCann remained philosophical; "If you get mentioned in the same breath as Ryan Giggs that can't be bad."

He's also wise enough in his 24-year-old head to realise that further opportunities for trophies and playing for his country will naturally appear as befitting his talent. Scotland can only benefit from his continuing growth and confidence. Hearts will hope to hold on to him as long as they possibly can.

Neil McCann statistics

Born: 11th August 1974

Height: 5' 10"

Weight: 10st

Previous Clubs:
  1991–96 Dundee
  1996— Heart of Midlothian

Hibernian

the hibees

Hibs confounded their critics by climbing to and holding the league lead for almost two months. Then it all went horribly wrong...

The Hibees delivered a lively and determined start to their league campaign. As if to exorcise the spirit of Darren Jackson and their previous over reliance on the Celtic-bound striker, Hibs recorded a convincing opening-day victory over the player's new club.

A spirited second-half fightback at Tannadice earned a well deserved draw and boosted the team's confidence to the degree that they convincingly crushed previous bugbears Kilmarnock 4–0. An expected defeat from city rivals Hearts did little to quell the new-found optimism at Easter Road, and Hibs enjoyed a convincing 5–2 pummelling of East End hardmen Dunfermline.

But that was it. From there on in, the Hibees fell down the league as, ironically, chairman Lex Gold became the spokesman for the new Scottish Super League. Bad luck rather than bad play seemed to characterise the team's fortunes until the visit of Rangers in October. Having taken the lead and held on to it for the first half, they added to their tally in the second and then, inexplicably, let the champions steal the game. It dented their confidence to the degree that the next six matches they played they lost. Jim Duffy tried to explain the poor form by saying: "When you are winning, things come off and when you aren't, they don't. When players are in that situation they are frightened to try things and maybe take two touches when previously they would have just taken one."

It needed more than two touches to save Hibs. One such was signing veteran striker Andy Walker from Sheffield United. He scored twice on his debut against Aberdeen and was more than unlucky not to score a hat-trick. If he had it would have been Hibs' first victory in ten games. Instead they had to settle for a draw.

The next touch was the sacking of Jim Duffy after a humiliating 6–2 defeat at the hands of Motherwell. Gold scoured the country for a new manager. Paul Sturrock was his first choice, but the St Johnstone board proved too wily to lose such an asset. A second attempt saw Lex approach Newcastle for Tommy Burns, but again the door was closed. Alex McLeish of Motherwell, jumped at the offer. As he visits places like Broadwood and Firhill next season, he'll probably wish he had stayed in the frying pan.

The only light spot in an otherwise gloomy season was the performance of the Hibs fans. Whether they turn out in such consistently high numbers for first division football remains to be seen.

CLUB FACTS	TRANSFERS IN			TRANSFERS OUT			
Stadium: Easter Road	6/97	Stephen Crawford	Millwall	£400k	6/97	Keith Wright	Raith Rovers	swap
0131 661 2159	6/97	Olafur Gottskalksson	Keflavik	£200k	3/98	Chic Charnley	Partick Thistle	Monthly
Capacity: 16,115	6/97	Anthony Rougier	Raith Rovers	£250k				
Managers: Jim Duffy, Alex McLeish	8/97	Jean Marc Boco	RC Lens	Free				
Club Captain: Willie Miller	2/98	Bryan Gunn	Norwich	nominal				
League Position in last five years:								
1992/93: 7th								
1993/94: 5th								
1994/95: 3rd								
1995/96: 5th								
1996/97: 9th								

GAME OF THE SEASON

January 31 1998

Motherwell (3) 6 Arnott 10, Weir 23, Garcin 43, McCulloch 81, Coyne 88
Hibernian (2) 2 Crawford 4, Lavety 8
Bookings: Falconer, Jackson, Dennis, Welsh
Attendance: 6,169 Referee: E Martindale

After seven minutes Hibs were two goals up. In the same space of time Motherwell equalised, to lead just before the interval. The second-half saw Motherwell dominate and add another three goals to their tally. On the back of a home cup loss to first division Raith Rovers, the fans finally got their wish – Jim Duffy was out of a job by Monday. The appointment of Alex McLeish soon followed.

Andy Dow in action

Barry Lavety

naughty boy

Bad luck has dogged a career of enormous promise, but despite a potentially crippling illness, the 'big silly boy' of Hibernian hit his best ever form this season.

The most surprising thing about the boy Lavety was that he was allowed to strut his stuff in the First Division with St Mirren for such an extended period before being snapped up for £200,000 in August 1996 by the then Hibernian manager Alex Miller.

Lavety had already made several successful Scotland Under 21 appearances, and in his first full season with St Mirren almost helped them make promotion to the Premier league in 1992–93. His scoring record approached an average of almost one goal in every two matches and saw him finish as one of the division's top scorers. He was widely tipped to go far.

In the same year and month that Duncan Ferguson was courting controversy by being sent to jail for a 'Glasgow kiss' on the field of play, Barry was embroiled in a little trouble of his own. A random drug test proved positive and, like the boy Ferguson, he found his liberty compromised when he was sent to a rehabilitation centre for drug takers.

"E's a naughty boy," taunted the tabloid screamers. His St Mirren manager at the time, Jimmy Bone, helped retain some perspective over the phoney outraged hoopla: "We can't condone what he has done, but we can't condemn him if it's a one-off and

he has just been a big silly boy." Lavety was, after all, only 21. The club disciplined him but he avoided dismissal when he explained that the positive substance had been a one-off experiment with a "social drug".

Bad luck seemed to follow him when, after scoring on his Hibs' debut, he was struck down by an arthritic condition which threatened his career; "I could hardly walk, let alone train," he said. Luckily for him, it was diagnosed as a virus. It put him out of the game for five months. He managed to make it back in time to help Hibs save themselves from the drop in last season's play-off deciders against Airdrie.

This season, his "big silly boy" tag came back to haunt him when he refused to move to St Johnstone after Jim Duffy had agreed to sell him to the Perthshire club. Duffy compromised and agreed to keep him if he could improve his play. That he did. Ironically he hit his best form after the departure of the outward bound manager.

His belief that Hibernian could beat the drop with only nine matches to go was helped by his crucial winning goal at Easter Road against fellow relegation strugglers Motherwell. His undoubted talent hasn't always come to the fore, but maybe a stint in the First Division

will give him enough of a kick to decide that it isn't the place where he should be trading his wares.

Barry Lavety statistics

Born: 21st Aug 1974

Height: 6ft

Weight: 12st 12lbs

Previous Clubs:
1991–96 St Mirren
1996— Hibernian

Kilmarnock

killie

Having finished the previous season as Scottish Cup winners and with a run of league form second only to Dundee United, Kilmarnock promised better things for the future.

For a team on a slow burn of continuous improvement since 1989 when second division football was their lot, Killie failed dismally in the first quarter of the Premier league.

Timidity in attack was exacerbated by a perforated defence. The successive meetings of title chasing trio Rangers, Hearts and Celtic saw Killie concede ten goals for no reply. Added to the 4–0 defeat by Hibernian and the team registered a goal difference of minus-13.

Yet, amazingly, the points tally accrued was the best they had ever recorded in the first quarter of the Premier Division. Testament, of a limited kind, to the management skills of Bobby Williamson. The season's fortunes turned when the defence was bolstered by the return of long-term injury victim and Scotland under-21 squad member, Jim Lauchlan. Described the previous season by media pundit

Tam Cowan as "Kilmarnock's secret weapon", the goal letting immediately stopped. The new solidity in defence was enhanced by the midfield creativity of a fully match-fit Pat Nevin, while a more forceful strikeforce was strengthened by the return of injury victim and Scotland B team international, Paul Wright – last season's highest scoring native striker.

It was no accident that Killie's improved team took them on a Premier record run of eight games without defeat. Fourth place, and a potential UEFA spot, was finally reached on the last game of 1997 against Hibernian. Killie became the only team in the whole of Europe to hold fourth position in any league with a negative goal difference – legacy of that poor start.

Attendances at home swelled, overtaking those of city-based team Dundee United. Killie were responsible

for some of the most entertaining and exciting matches in the league. None more so than those against title pretenders Hearts. In the face of a myopically polarised Scottish media, it was the English based newspapers such as the Times, Telegraph, Mail, and Express who continually acknowledged the finer points of Kilmarnock's play.

Before the season started, manager Bobby Williamson said: "If I had a million quid to spend, it would be us that were chasing Rangers and Celtic, not Dundee United." Like every provincial club in Scotland, Kilmarnock are under-resourced and undervalued. If Scotland ever wants to regain the footballing credibility it possessed ten years ago it should hope that more teams like Kilmarnock get their proverbial million quid.

GAME OF THE SEASON

January 3 1998

Kilmarnock (3) 4 Wright 8; 33, Mitchell 44, Roberts 88
Motherwell (1) 1 Coyne 24
Bookings: McMillan, Philliben, Weir, Coyne
MacPherson (75 Sent Off)
Attendance: 8,724 Referee: M McCurry

Motherwell bore the brunt of the Rugby Park revolution in this storm-lashed game. Outplayed, out-fought and out-thought, the game brought home to the visitors that unlike previous seasons, Killie could no longer be considered points in the bag. The result was Killie's highest scoring victory in a five-month home period in which they lost no matches.

CLUB FACTS	TRANSFERS IN			TRANSFERS OUT		
Stadium: **Rugby Park**	**Martin Baker**	Saint Mirren	£175,000	**Dragoje Lekovic**	Sporting Gijon	
01563 525184	**Jerome Vareille**	FC Mulhouse	free	**Colin McKee**	various	
Capacity: 18,200	**Pat Nevin**	Tranmere Rovers	£65,000	**Neil Whitworth**	Wigan Athletic	
Manager: **Bobby Williamson**	**Gordon Marshall**	Celtic	£150,000	**Jim MacIntyre**	Reading	£500,000
Club Captain: **Ray Montgomerie**						
League Position in last five years:						
1992-93: 2nd (1st Division)						
1993-94: 8th						
1994-95: 7th						
1995-96: 7th						
1996-97: 7th						

The more forceful strikeforce was strengthened by the return of Paul Wright – last season's highest scoring native international striker.

Allsport

Paul Wright

a light in a bushel

Recognition has been a long time coming for this Kilmarnock giant, but he's taken to international duty as easily as he has any other task in football.

When Kilmarnock faced Saint Johnstone at McDiarmid Park in the final match between the two teams this season, Paul Wright had already played a mid-week match for the Scotland B team against Wales. In keeping with the potential of the player, he scored.

The match programme congratulated Paul for the call up and promptly added; "When Paul was a Saints player we argued that he was good enough to be capped. If he'd been with a more 'fashionable' club at that time there is little doubt that he would have been given his chance at international level."

It was a moot point. The programme then used the example of Billy Dodds, another ex-Saints player, who transferred to Aberdeen; "...is that not what happened with Billy Dodds, who certainly isn't a better player than Paul."

Rumours abound as to why Wright continually failed to be called up or even managed to achieve the media recognition he deserved. Last season he scored crucial goals in both of Kilmarnock's March victories over the Old Firm, yet it scarcely raised a ripple of interest outside of Ayrshire. Only his solitary winning goal in the Scottish Cup final seemed to merit the attention the player deserved, yet his league

performance was arguably more impressive – he was the highest scoring native player in the Scottish Premier League.

Again, this season, his 100th Premier goal scored against Rangers – only the 13th player to have achieved such a record – was overshadowed by a serious head injury sustained by Gordon Durie. Unlucky for some.

While at Hibernian Wright scored on his debut against Hearts only to suffer an injury which put him out of the game for five months. He finished the season with a tally of six goals which still managed to see him hit the record books as the top scorer for Hibs in 1990–91.

While with St Johnstone he scored 42 goals in 80 games and from 1991–94 was the team's top scorer. A cruciate ligament injury robbed him of matches for an 18-month period. In that injury time, the rude sacking of Alex Totten from the Perthshire side left him considered as excess baggage by incoming manager Paul Sturrock.

Totten snapped him up for his new and present club, Kilmarnock, in March 1995. Again, Wright finished as his chosen club's top scorer in the three full seasons he's played since joining the team. Such consistency in front of goal is no accident. His speed of

thought is matched by a deftness of touch and a blistering shot which can see goals conjured out of nothing. As unsung heroes go, a Scotland B international before the main symphony of the World Cup is a bum note to end the season on. Here's hoping that Craig Brown suffers for his intransigence at not exploiting one of Scotland's brighter goalscoring stars. It is to Brown's detriment that Paul Wright hasn't been better used.

Paul Wright statistics

Born: 17th August 67

Height: 5' 8"

Weight: 11st 7lbs

Previous Clubs:
  1983–89 Aberdeen
  1989–90 Queens Park Rangers
  1990–91 Hibernian
  1991–95 Saint Johnstone
  1995—   Kilmarnock

Motherwell

the well

Lacklustre performances and a dispirited atmosphere led to a horrific season which Well's supporters will remember for all the wrong reasons.

There was a period, during and after the departure of ex-Well manager Tommy McLean, when Motherwell were considered one of the most exciting teams to watch in Scotland.

Flair, confidence, skill and a burning belief in the ascendancy of provincialism brought the club into the realm of forceful credibility. McLean had managed to take them to a creditable third place in the 1993–94 season. His legacy left the incoming Alex McLeish with an inheritance enabling him to go one step further and claim runners-up spot the following season.

Well fans looked forward to the future with condence. It was a future that never came. This season, like the previous two, brought the stark reality to Fir Park that the club is in terminal decline. With Alex McLeish's departure

it looks as if Premier League survival is the best accolade they can hope to achieve for the foreseeable future.

There are many reasons for this sad drop in fortune; lack of resources, unsound transfers, an ageing squad, an inspirationally challenged manager, poor investment, and general apathy. Taken singly, any one of these maladies can bring down a team. Combined, the concoction may yet poison the club.

This season saw Motherwell make their worst Premier start in 12 years. The poor start continued throughout the season with Well unable to find any kind of rhythm. Ironically, the only team they mustered consistently worthwhile performances against were Rangers, taking seven from a possible 12 points. Their reputation for attractive football, just like Alex MacLeish, has disappeared over the

horizon. The millstone of relegation hung round their sorry necks almost from the first month.

McLeish's February departure from Fir Park to Easter Road is most notable due to the well publicised fact that he was third choice, behind Paul Sturrock and Tommy Burns, for a Hibernian team also wallowing at the league's bottom.

Whether Well's new, mostly unknown, manager Harri Kampman can turn things around is a question many provincial clubs will want to see answered positively. It will be to the impoverishment of Scottish football if he can't.

CLUB FACTS

Stadium: Fir Park
  (01698) 333 333
Capacity: 13,742
Manager: Alex McLeish, Harri Kampman
Club Captain: Brian Martin
League Position in last five years:
1992-93: 9th
1993-94: 3rd
1994-95: 2nd
1995-96: 8th
1996-97: 8th

TRANSFERS IN

8/97	Eliphas Shivute	Eleven Arrows	£100k
1/98	Eric Garcin	Lille	free
3/98	Stefan Lindqvist	Gothenburg	£125k

TRANSFERS OUT

9/97	Scott Howey	Reading	£30k
10/97	Franz Resch	Darlington	Free
10/97	Mario Dorner	Darlington	Free

GAME OF THE SEASON

21st March 1998
Hibernian (1) 1 Lavety 34
Motherwell (0) 0
Bookings: Martin, Falconer, Coyle, Valikarri
Elliot (sent off)
Attendance: 10,582 Referee: S Dougal

The first game against Well's ex-manager was always going to be a test of mettle and resolve. It was also a relegation six pointer. Having disposed of the Champions a week before, Motherwell were favourites to beat hapless Hibernian. Characterising the schizophrenic nightmare of their season, the Well lost to a lesser team. It ensured a tense and edgy end to the season.

Photo News Scotland

With Alex McLeish's departure it looks
as if Premier League survival is the best
accolade Motherwell can hope to achieve
for the foreseeable future.

Tommy Coyne

coyning it in

Motherwell's veteran goalscoring interntional is approaching an age when pundits want to write him off, but his continuing importance to the club is undeniable.

When Tommy Coyne was signed for Motherwell from Tranmere Rovers in 1993, the home fans were less than ecstatic: "Tommy was one of those players that we could never take to when he played for anybody else," was the word on the terraces.

Yet his arrival coincided with a complete revival of the Motherwell footballing machine and their respective fortunes in the league – 3rd in 1993–94 and 2nd in 1994–95. The fans were quickly won over

Coyne's career has always been punctuated with prolific goal scoring. His leanest spell occurred while with Dundee United and was transformed just across the road at Dens Park, the home of Dundee. 33 goals in 43 Premier matches in the 1987/88 season with the Dark Blues still stands to this day in the Premier League record books.

His goalscoring exploits with Dundee soon found Glasgow Celtic knocking on the door. The half million Celtic investment took a couple of seasons to be paid back in terms of goal returns. Celtic fans, when asked about Coyne quickly point to the hat trick he scored against Hearts in their opening game of season 1989–90 as a thing of beauty. Coyne's undoubted footballing ability and deadly striking skills are augmented by a keen intelligence and

exceptional work rate. It is a point of pride in Motherwell that while playing there Coyne was selected to play for the Republic of Ireland no less than 13 times. Jack Charlton's game plan for the Republic was never a secret. Coyne's inclusion in the World Cup squad fitted it perfectly. He took part in the World Cup victory over Italy in 1994 and still cites that match as the most memorable he has ever played in. He is still the only Motherwell player ever to have taken part in a World Cup campaign.

Injury held back the number of domestic appearances he made in the 1995/96 and 1996/97 seasons, and it's probably no coincidence that this happened along with a drop in league form that resulted in Motherwell being deeply drawn into the relegation dogfight.

Critics are keen to write him off as he approaches his 36th year. The depth of understanding and almost telepathic relationship he's developed with fellow Irish international Owen Coyle, has however allowed him to offset his loss of pace and could still see him plundering goals for some seasons yet.

Such is the importance of Tommy Coyne to Motherwell that his loss could be a mortal blow from which the club might never recover.

Tommy Coyne statistics

Born: 14th October 1962, Glasgow

Height: 6ft

Weight: 10st 7lb

Previous Clubs:
- 1981–83 Clydebank
- 1983–86 Dundee United
- 1986–88 Dundee
- 1988–92 Celtic
- 1992–93 Tranmere Rovers
- 1993— Motherwell

Rangers

the gers

Rangers stumbled from drama to crisis. Shaky in defence, only Marco Negri's assassin's skills kept them in the race. When the Italian's talent failed him the team were left not knowing what to do.

Before his pre-season £15 million spend, Walter Smith would have done well to have studied Machiavelli. Particularly his warning on mercenaries of war: "...if one holds his state based on these arms, he will stand neither firm or safe; for they are disunited, ambitious and without discipline, unfaithful, valiant before friends, cowardly before enemies."

Machiavelli may have been a Lazio fan when he penned this, but the kingdom of Ibrox was to reverberate throughout the season to its implications. That titles can be won by mercenaries was proved by Marco Negri in front of goal whose performance up to December won Rangers enough games to keep them consistently in the top three of the league.

Nevertheless, the Gers stood neither firm nor safe due to their inability to win more than two games in a row.

Particularly negligent was the undisciplined performance of their defence. Unlike previous championship winning seasons, disunited mistakes riddled their play. The first sign of panic from Walter appeared through the October re-signing of tired veteran defender Richard Gough.

Gough proved more of a liability than a saviour with increasingly brutal fouls. Luckily for him, most referees proved myopically benevolent until Kenny Clark showed character in the crucial February Ibrox match between second place Hearts and third place Rangers. Gough was sent off for a second bookable offence. Afterwards some pundits even called for a change in the rules.

Unfaithful ambition cropped up when Danish international Brian Laudrup, wilting under the pressure of being expected to carry a listless team,

secured a deal which saw him heading in the direction of Chelsea. Unsurprisingly, the flair of the Dane never quite found the creative output or effectiveness of previous seasons.

The offloading of Paul Gascoigne to Premiership bound Middlesborough proved to be the one masterstroke that the club carried out. The team began functioning more as a unit and for the first time in the league campaign put together a string of six victories in a row. It was also notable that this was partly due to the inclusion of the old hands like McCoist and McCall who played for the jersey.

When Dick Advocaat takes over for the new season, it is to be hoped that he will at least pay lip service to the fact that Rangers play in Scotland.

GAME OF THE SEASON
2 May 1998
Rangers 0 (0)
Kilmarnock 1 (0) Mitchell 90
Bookings: Marshall
Attendance: 50116 Referee: B Tait (East Kilbride)
The last ever home match for Walter Smith and several of the Ibrox stars was set to be a gala day. Victory would put the team at the top of the table and increase the pressure on Celtic who had already slipped up in similar circumstances in the past. Sadly, it wasn't to be. In front of the biggest crowd of the season, Kilmarnock proved too resilient and in the third minute of stoppage time effectively killed off the Ibrox club's chance of making history.

CLUB FACTS

Stadium: **Ibrox**
Capacity: **50,411**
Manager: **Walter Smith**
Club Captain: **Richard Gough**
League Position in last five seasons:
1992/93: 1st
1993/94: 1st
1994/95: 1st
1995/96: 1st
1996/97: 1st

TRANSFERS IN

Date	Player	From	Fee
6/97	Lorenzo Amoruso	Fiorentina	£4m
6/97	Gennaro Gattuso	Perugia AC Spa	Free
6/97	Marco Negri	Perugia AC Spa	£3.7m
6/97	Antti Niemi	FC Copenhagen A/S	ND
6/97	Sergio Porrini	Juventus FC Spa	£3m
6/97	Stale Stensaas	Rosenborg BK	£1.5m
6/97	Jonas Thern	AS Roma	£1.5m
6/97	Antony Vidmar	NAC Breda	£1m
8/97	Jonatan Johansson	FC Flora	£1m

TRANSFERS OUT

Date	Player	To	Fee
6/97	Greg Shields	Dunfermline	£175k
9/97	Andy Dibble	Luton	Monthly
9/97	Mark Hateley	Hull City	Free
11/97	Brian McGinty	Hull City	Monthly
3/98	Paul Gascoigne	Middlesbrough	£3.45m
3/98	Gary Bollan	St Johnstone	£100k

Alex Clelland outruns Jackie McNamara in the dispiriting 2–0 defeat for Rangers on 2nd January.

Marco Negri

a true star

In a season of mixed fortunes and early uncertain form, Marco Negri's killer instinct in the first half of the campaign was often the only reason Rangers stayed in the running.

Marco Negri managed to slot 30 goals past some of the best defences in the country, and that was before half the season was done. When Marco Negri, sometimes referred to as Marco Goalo, joined Rangers from ex-Serie A team Perugia, he was mostly unknown. Certainly in the British Isles.

The situation didn't last long. In his first nine league games for Rangers he smashed the previous record of Ally MacLeod of Hibernian set in 1977–78 of scoring in eight consecutive matches – the best run by a Premier player since its inception in 1975. Marco scored in his first nine games in a row, a somewhat ominous figure for Rangers. His solitary goal in the Bears' first defeat at Tannadice in October matched the Ranger's record of a player scoring in nine consecutive games set in the 1920–21 season by Andy Cunningham.

In his tenth league match, the man-marking attention of Celtic's Danish international Marc Rieper cancelled out Negri's threat. But the Dane's distracted attention let Richard Gough sneak in to a virtually impregnable Celtic defence and score the only goal of the two team's first meeting of the season at Ibrox.

Curiously, though, rather than concentrating on the goal producing talent of the Italian, the media focused more on his low key verging on no-key goal celebrations. Unlike the pretentiously deceptive jersey kissing of so many foreign legion Old Firm stars, Negri if anything looked unhappy about scoring. A phenomenon he conceded to: "It was because I had problems."

Understandably, the problems ranged from everything to the house he lived in to the language he spoke to the right-hand-drive car he had to get to work; "I would not get to bed until one o'clock in the morning, and then I would just lie there, wide awake all night, worrying about my problems, and realising that I was not happy."

Ironically, as he became happier, the goals dried up. By the end of December and the end of his particularly unhappy problematic period, he had scored 30 league goals. By the end of April, only two more goals were added to this tally. Unsurprisingly Negri found himself increasingly unused. The increasing pressure on Rangers to achieve their historic ten in a row dream couldn't afford a non-performing sultry Italian passenger.

The unhappy ending for the Italian can't hide the fact that were it not for his goalscoring exploits, Rangers would not even have been in the hunt for the title. By the end of March, his tally accounted for half of all the goals Rangers had scored throughout the season.

An unignorable total and one which brought him to the attention of the Italian media and the international coaching crew. Whether Negri will be with Rangers next season remains to be seen, but nothing can take away from an outstanding first half of the season. A true star.

Marco Negri statistics

Born: 27th October 1970

Height: 5' 11.5"

Weight: 12st 10lbs

Previous Clubs:
1994–95 Cosenza
1995–97 Perugia
1997— Glasgow Rangers

St Johnstone

the saints

The Saints managed more than their fair share of glory with their historic January victory over Rangers which rubber-stamped their Premier Division credentials for the new millennium.

Despite St Johnstone's all-time Scottish First Division record accumulation of 80 points in the 1996–97 season, and a defensive record that included 20 league shutouts, they were still the bookies favourites to face the drop.

Paul Sturrock and his team of journeymen, however, had very different ideas from the bookies. Their strategic adherence to shape, composure, organisation, and work rate ensured that St Johnstone were never overrun or intimidated by supposedly superior opposition. Indeed, no team managed to beat St Johnstone by more than a two-goal differential throughout their Premier campaign – testament to the solidity of their defence and midfield and the players' willingness to help each other out when faced with adversity. It is well known that Sturrock has no time for players perceived as shirkers.

While hardly inspirational or spectator-friendly, the Saints still managed to engage in more than their fair share of provisional glory. In a five-week period spanning the end of December to the end of January, they put both Old Firm title challengers to the sword at McDiarmid Park. And, again at McDiarmid, had it not been for a resilient and plucky fightback from the pretenders to the title, Heart of Midlothian, Saints could have recorded five straight victories in a row.

A drop in form followed the transfer of their highly talented ex-youth team left-back, Callum Davidson. Departing for Blackburn Rovers at a premium price of £1,750,000, his last match saw him contribute to the team's historic 2–0 victory over Rangers. It was the Saints' first victory over the Glasgow club in 27 years and it rubber-stamped their Premier Division credentials for the new millennium.

If Sturrock can find his much sought for clinical finishers, then there's no doubt that his team will grow into a force to be feared, if not necessarily admired, throughout the land.

CLUB FACTS

Stadium: **McDiarmid Park**
    (01783) 626961
Capacity: **10,673**
Manager: **Paul Sturrock**
Team Captain: **Jim Weir**
League Position in last five years:
1992-93 6th
1993-94 10th
1994-95 5th (First Division)
1995-96 4th (First Division)
1996-97 1st (First Division)

TRANSFERS IN

Date	Player	From	Fee
6/97	Paul Kane	Viking FK	Free
1/98	Paddy Connolly	Airdrie	£250k
3/98	Tommy Wright	Airdrie	£150k
2/98	Davide Xausa	Stoke	Free
3/98	Gary Bollan	Rangers	£100k
3/98	Gerry McMahon	Tottenham Hotspur	£85k

TRANSFERS OUT

Date	Player	To	Fee
2/98	Callum Davidson	Blackburn Rovers	£1.75m

GAME OF THE SEASON

January 31st 1998
St Johnstone (1) 2 O'Neil 36, Boyle 69
Rangers (0) 0
Bookings: None
Attendance: 10,436 Referee: J McCluskey

If ever there was a match to dispel the myth that newly promoted St Johnstone would be points fodder for the rest of the league, this was it. St Johnstone called the shots with superior organisation and mature play belying their humble resources. They made the reigning champions look ordinary and shambolic. A warning to the rest of the league.

Photo News Scotland

A warning to the rest of the league:
despite humble resources in comparison
to their opponents, the Saints made
Rangers look shambolic at the very end
of January.

Photo News Scotland

Alan Main

main man saves the day

The Saints won themselves an international when Alan Main's capabilities were finally recognised by the Scotland selectors, something Paul Sturrock could have told them about years before.

E verything about my game is totally different from what it was before," stated keeper Alan Main in an interview to explain his unbelievable first quarter of the season showing against Aberdeen at Pittodrie, and Kilmarnock at Rugby Park.

St Johnstone recorded three victories in this first quarter. Two of the games were played away, and all of them were won by a 1–0 scoreline. After the match against Kilmarnock several Sunday papers awarded Main the unprecedented mark of ten out of ten for his performance.

All three victories ended with St Johnstone's collective backs to the wall in scenes reminiscent of the Alamo. Main took charge of his goal as if the team's lives depended on the result and pulled off saves that left the opposition players and fans gasping "how did he do that?"

His confidence was further boosted in October when he was called up by Scotland, in preference to Celtic's Jonathan Gould, for the World Cup qualifier against Latvia. Justifying the order of the choice, Craig Brown said: "He [Gould] has done very well since he came here, but we've got to acknowledge the superb season Alan Main had last season. I know Alan very well and I know his capabilities."

Main became the first player from the Perth club for nearly 70 years to receive a Scotland call-up

Season 1996–97 was testament to the reliability of Main. In a programme consisting of 36 games, he recorded a clean sheet in 20 of them. Furthermore, ten of these clean sheets were achieved consecutively.

One man who wasn't surprised by all the fuss and hoopla surrounding Main was his manager, Paul Sturrock: "No one's listened to me but Alan's been doing the same for two-and-a-half years now." Born in Elgin in 1967, Main first played for Elgin City before being snapped up by Dundee United in 1986. First-team football with the the Tangerines mostly eluded him until, after a loan period with Cowdenbeath and East Stirling, season 1989–90 beckoned.

A fairly full, if undistinguished, programme followed until 1993–94, Dundee United's Scottish Cup-winning season when Main was gradually eased out of the Tannadice first eleven. St Johnstone stepped in for him in 1995 when he became an integral component of the Paul Sturrock revolution sweeping through MacDiarmid Park.

With Main in his 30th year, he acknowledges that in the tradition of

Alan David Main statistics

Born: 5th December 67

Height: 6ft

Weight: 11st

Previous Clubs:
1986–89	Dundee United
1988–89	Cowdenbeath
1988–89	East Stirlingshire
1989–94	Dundee United
1994—	Saint Johnstone

fine wine, cheese, and goalkeepers he should be getting better with age: "I can still further improve on what I am doing. If I keep on improving I have got a chance. But there is a lot more hard work to be done."

Opposition strikers should take note.

Other Competitions
home and away

With the change in the rules concerning the number of teams eligible for entry to the various European competitions, Scotland fared average to middling.

T he Champions League had to be qualified for over two legs. Rangers, Scotland's representatives, didn't quite manage to make the league, but due to the increased number of entrants, they were allowed a second chance, so to speak, in the UEFA Cup competition.

UEFA, is probably the most difficult trophy to win due to the number of entrants. A minor battle of Britain occurred in the first round in this competition due to the meeting of Celtic and Liverpool. Celtic went out to the Anfield Reds, who later lost out to the team who knocked out Rangers – RC Strasbourg.

The Cup Winners' Cup was looked upon as a diminished tournament. Due to the extra number of entrants allowed into the Champions League, some of the teams who had won cups in their respective countries, had also attained runner-up positions in their home leagues. This allowed them entry to the more financially lucrative Champions League, and naturally they chose the fiscally advantageous route.

Bursting to break in to the big time were Dundee. Not only did they run away with the Scottish First Division, they also showed that they could mix it with the big boys when they forced a draw against Rangers at Ibrox and were narrowly beaten in a replay at their home ground, Dens Park.

Like birds in flight: Liverpool's Stig Inge Bjornebye and Celtic's Morten Wieghorst scrap for a 2–2 draw in the UEFA Cup Round 1, 16th September.

Action Images

Cup Winners' Cup

Their first Euro outing in 26 years proved to be a bit of disaster for Scottish Cup holders Kilmarnock. Their loss of form at the wrong moment proved to be their undoing in a competion that was there for the taking.

Success for us here at Kilmarnock is not about promotion to the First or Premier Divisions, it is about returning to European football and that is our aim." Thus wrote Bobby Fleeting, then chairman of Kilmarnock football club in 1994. Universal catcalls of "ideas above their station" and "get a grip on reality" met Kilmarnock and the club's supporters. The 1960s and 70s were the last time Killie played European football.

The return to Europe occurred under the most unlikely of circumstances. Season 1996–97, despite the best squad Kilmarnock had assembled in 20 years, produced a first-half league performance which left the Ayrshire team rock bottom and relegation favourites.

But still the European dream burned bright, at least among the fans. The sacking of then manager Alex Totten, left the club under the caretakership of ex-Kilmarnock striker Bobby Williamson. And almost immediately, positive results began to be achieved on the field of play.

Belief washed over the club and found eloquent expression in the Scottish Cup. Killie barnstormed their way to the final and beat off a battling Falkirk who belied their First Division

status. European football beckoned.

Quite what happened during the summer break, no one will ever know, but the coherency and cohesion of the team deserted them just when they needed it most. Their opening game in the European Cup Winners' Cup in August was a qualifier that saw them snatch an undeserved victory at home against a plucky Shelbourne.

The return match at Shelbourne's Tolka Park in Dublin was more of the same for Killie. The Irishmen ran them ragged and were unlucky not to take all three points from what ended up as a 1–1 draw. Killmarnock were through... but only just.

The first round proper threw up a tie against OGC Nice. Recently relegated to the French Second Division, the management had jettisoned the majority of their big-name stars. Playing in France in the middle of September, Kilmarnock's lacklustre performance flattered the mediocre French team. The away goal in their 3–1 defeat gave the Ayrshiremen a fighting chance – although the fight in them had been posted missing since the start of August.

The return leg witnessed Kilmarnock as the last Scottish team in Europe. This time they didn't disgrace

themselves. An immaculately aggressive game produced little skill but plenty of excitement. Killie opened the scoring through the tenacious Reilly and for a long period of the game the fans and team seemed to believe they could do it. The belief was cruelly dashed 14 minutes from time when, throwing caution to the wind, Killie were caught by a sucker punch.

Accepting that they had learned from the experience, Killie vowed to get into Europe again at the first opportunity.

Playing in France in the middle of September, Kilmarnock's lacklustre performance flattered the mediocre OGC Nice.

PREMIERSHIP WINNERS

European Cup

The mini-battle of Britain between Celtic and Liverpool was as nothing compared to the battle faced by Dundee United – the Tangerine Terrors – in Turkey. Beaten but not cowed, they did Britain proud.

The qualifying round of the UEFA cup witnessed a clinically ruthless assassination of Andorran amateurs CE Principat by Dundee United. Seventeen goals scored over two legs almost but not quite matched the highest scoring aggregate of 21 in the competition set by Chelsea and Feyenoord respectively.

The ease with which the club made their qualifying entry had its mirror opposite in the first round against Trabzonspor in Turkey. Faced with a frighteningly hostile home crowd under a humidity blanket set at 70 degrees plus, the team had to draw on all their reserves of physical and mental courage and conviction.

It was almost enough. But they figured without the foibles of a German referee who awarded the home side a dubious penalty 13 minutes from time. The spot kick was duly converted by the highly skilful Miniran Hami whose shots throughout the match had peppered and harassed the United goal.

The disappointing result offered United hope that they could do the business at home. Sweeping changes from the side who had suffered a 5–1 humiliation at the hands of Rangers produced some incisively devastating attacks. The inability to convert the moves into goals was finally overcome in the second half when a pinpoint cross was converted by a powerful header from Alan MacLaren. Alas, Hami popped up again to steal the tie nine minutes from time. United were out but they could hold their heads high.

Celtic's qualifier was a much different story from that of United. Up against Welsh part-timers Inter Cable-Tel, the Glasgow team struggled to impose their superiority. The scoreline of 3–0 to Celtic was dissatisfying for Wim Jansen, Celtic's new Dutch coach.

The second leg in Glasgow proved to be nothing more than a training match that saw the Glasgow giants strolling to a 5–0 victory. The next round proper proved much more of a challenge.

Liverpool, history's European giants and present season's creditable Premiership challengers were expected to walk all over the Scottish team. The predictions looked like following the formbook when the overwhelming first half dominance of the English side seemed intent on crushing all resistance from the hapless Celts. An early Michael Owen goal provided scant reward for the Englishmen's efforts. A second-half deluge was expected. Surprisingly, the tables were turned. Celtic raised their game a couple of notches and overcame Liverpool.

Jackie McNamara proved instrumental in the resurgence when a splendidly worked one-two with Craig Burley resulted in a terrific equaliser. The continuous harrying of the Liverpool defence by Simon Donnelly finally resulted in a penalty that was duly converted. Only a late injury-time equaliser from Steve McManaman put Liverpool in the driving seat for the second leg a fortnight later.

The return leg proved difficult for the Anfielders but they did enough to hold Celtic to a non-scoring draw. If nothing else, both matches did much to alleviate the needless inferiority complex Scots suffer concerning their Southern brothers' allegedly superior football.

Karl-Heinz Riedle performs a Liverpool Leap over Celtic's Stephane Mahe.

Action Images

Champions' League

Despite total domination on the domestic front, Rangers had always found it tough in the European scene. A team still learning to gel with each other narrowly failed to make headway.

Rangers. A big club. A powerful club. A glorious club. A club which vies with Liverpool and Manchester United for the title of Britain's grandest and most successful club. A club which dominates Scottish football to the degree that the only credible challenge to their overwhelming superiority can come from Europe.

Rangers. A forward looking club whose grandiose vision of a European Super League with their team at the helm set the fan's imaginations on fire.

This season's European performance from the Gers almost made up for some of the heroically unlucky misfortunes of the past. A 15 million strengthening of the team narrowly failed to achieve much sought for European glory. In the Champions League preliminary qualifier, facing Faroe Island giants GI Gotu, Walter Smith's men sailed through both legs with an electrifying display of football. The aggregate score of 11–0 to the Gers flattered the Faroe Islanders. Suitably encouraged, Rangers' loyal and faithful fans were ecstatic. They could hardly wait for the next match in Sweden against Swedish champions IFK Gothenburg.

Partisan, interested, and neutral parties listening to the match commentary from famously impartial BBC Radio Scotland were treated to a match full of "brilliant" Rangers passing, "fantastic" Rangers movement, and "terrific" Rangers shots. Astoundingly though, the gritty and highly organised IFK managed to absorb this "super" performance, netting three lucky goals against the run of play.

The return leg at Ibrox produced a spirited and defiant show of football from the Scottish Champions but it wasn't quite enough to break down the compact and unified Swedes. The Gers had to settle for a respectable draw. They could hold their heads high with Euro pride.

Fortunately for the club, the story didn't end with the exit from the financially lucrative Champions League. Due to changes in tournament rules, the Gers were given a second chance to derive even more respect through the vehicle of the UEFA Cup. Lamentably, they weren't quite up to the task. RC Strasbourg, challenging for the bottom spot in the French First Division, raised their game several notches and harried Rangers with devastating counter attacks. Somehow, they forced a competent Rangers' defence into conceding two penalties. The Gers' consolation away goal, however, provided them with a lifeline to take back to fortress Ibrox.

Again, bad luck rather than bad play dogged their Euro aspirations. Despite taking an early lead at Ibrox and looking like they were going through to the next round, a lapse of concentration let them down. Strasbourg equalised close to half time. In the second half, with Rangers hunting in packs, the French team hit them with a classic counter attack to end yet another so near but so far Euro dream.

Rangers' Stale Stensaas tussles with Stefan Petterson of Gothenburg in the 1–1 draw for the Champions League qualifier, 27th August.

PREMIER WINNERS

Scottish FA Cup

By the semi-final stage, three of the teams in this year's cup could have won the double of the League and Cup. One could even have won the treble. But you could never discount Rangers.

In keeping with the thrilling league title race, the Scottish Cup threw up more than its fair share of romance, drama, tension, upset and excitement.

In a way, it was like a microcosm of the league itself. All three title-chasing teams, Rangers, Hearts and Celtic made it to the semi-final, with Falkirk, beaten finalists from the previous year, adding the romantic wildcard.

Hearts had the easiest run, disposing of Second Division Clydebank, Third Division Alloa, and First Division relegation material, Ayr United. Each team had an expected flurry but the superiority of the Edinburgh club soon came to the fore.

Celtic encountered and knocked out two Premier teams, Dunfermline in the fourth round and Dundee United in the quarter-final. The victory over United was achieved in the cruellest of fashions. Erik Pedersen, United's stalwart defender, knocked in an own goal in the dyeing seconds of the match. His face was the personification of disbelief and disappointment.

Rangers had the shakiest performance on the road to the semi-final. Their first match against homeless First Division Hamilton Academicals was saved by Richard Gough in stoppage time. Their first Premier opposition, Motherwell, looked to have the match wrapped up when a poor mistake by 'Well keeper Chris Woods let Gordon Durie steal an equaliser. The replay at Ibrox was won resoundingly by the Gers. A stuttering home performance against First Division champions Dundee resulted in a dull goalless draw. The talismanic McCoist put the replay beyond Dundee at Dens Park and Rangers into the semi.

While the title-chasers were proving a point, Falkirk provided the romance. But behind their cavalier performance lay potential disaster. The players agreed to take a wage cut so that the club – up to its eyes in debt – could continue to function. An expected victory over local rivals Stenhousemuir at Ochilview saw them having to travel to Kirkcaldy to face deadly league rivals Raith Rovers who had been responsible for the dismissal of Hibs in the earlier rounds. A closely fought match resulted in the flattering score of 3–1 to Falkirk.

The first big test came against Premier team St Johnstone at Falkirk's crumbling home ground Brockville. For the first time in the season, St Johnstone lost by more than two goals. Falkirk were thoroughly deserving of the win and looked forward to a semi-final pay off which would help the club's financial problems.

The semi-final draw saw the Old Firm pitted against each other. Rangers triumphed. They absorbed everything Celtic could fire at them and punished the mistakes of the Hoops to win 2–1.

Falkirk put on a fiery dominant display against Hearts at Ibrox but lacked the firepower to make it count. Kevin McAllister's solo performance ranked as one of the best of any player throughout the season. His wonder-equaliser deserved to win the match. Alas, Neil McCann punished the Bairns on the break. There was to be no repeat of last year's heroic struggle against Celtic. The final was between Rangers and Hearts.

Photo News Scotland

In the semi-final, Celtic went down 2–1
to Rangers, leaving the final battle
between the Gers and Hearts.

Division One

How would you feel when at the height of your success you were sacked for not fitting in with the board's way of doing things? That's exactly what happened to the manager of Dundee.

It's widely expected that Hibernian will bounce back to the new super league in one season. Anyone with more than a passing acquaintance with the First Division knows that this isn't quite the certainty it is mooted to be.

Despite the fact that First Division champions and Super League-bound Dundee broke free of the pack and maintained their substantial lead for over half the season, the difference between most of the teams in the division is cosmetic. It does not provide the quality of the Premier, but it is certainly more competitive and exciting, providing more entertainment than its mostly predictable Premier brother.

The biggest handicap facing the teams is a fiscal one. Crowds for the better supported clubs, such as Dundee, rarely break the 4,000 mark and the lack of hard cash means that even when a team does make it to the Premier, the odds are stacked against it surviving more than two seasons.

Several clubs were, and are, on the verge of folding. Partick Thistle were only saved by the benevolence of their creditors and a successfully high-profile 'Save the Jags' campaign which saw fashionable celebrity supporters come out of the woodwork.

More deserving yet more likely to lose out through the higher league's reconstruction are Falkirk. Yet again they proved that they are more than capable of mixing it with the big boys when, for the second year running, they reached the Scottish Cup semi-final. Falkirk have the distinction of being the only team in Scotland to have beaten the highly organised Premier side St Johnstone by more than a two-goal differential. Their runners-up spot which would normally have afforded a play-off place is allegedly being compensated for with a payment of £250,000. Like many of the features boasted of for the new Scottish super league, the payment will only be believed when it is paid into Falkirk's bank account.

Most of the Premier clubs have been taken over by businessmen and consortiums whose style of business practice was typified by the board of Dundee. John McCormack, the manager who had assembled the youthful Dundonian side which by February had raced to a five-point lead in the division, was sacked in the same month. It was explained by the club's board that "he didn't fit in with the present set up". How the most successful manager in the division with the most successful team didn't fit in made the mind boggle. But it didn't change the course of events.

Jocky Scott, ex-manager of Dundee ten years previously had a face which did fit in with the present set-up. Whether or not Dundee can mix it in the new higher league remains to be seen. Their Scottish Cup quarter-final performance against Rangers, where they forced a replay at Ibrox, suggests that they can. The credit lies firmly at the door of John McCormack.

Having roundly beaten league rivals Raith Rovers 3–1, Falkirk faced Premier team St Johnstone. For the first time in the season, St Johnstone lost by more than two goals. Falkirk were thoroughly deserving of the win and looked forward to a semi-final pay off which would help the club's financial problems.

Photo News Scotland

Allsport

MONTH-BY-MONTH, BLOW-BY-BLOW GUIDE TO THE PREMIERSHIP

DATE	TEAMS & SCORES	GOALSCORERS	Booked	Sent Off
2/8/97	Aberdeen (0) 0 / Kilmarnock (0) 0		4	0
2/8/97	Dunfermline (0) 0 / Motherwell (0) 2	Coyne 63 pen, 85	5	0
2/8/97	St Johnstone (0) 1 / Dundee Utd (1) 1	McKimmie 61 og / Olofsson 11	3	0
3/8/97	Hibernian (1) 2 / Celtic (1) 1	Charnley 75, Power 24 / MacKay 29	3	0
3/8/97	Rangers (2) 3 / Hearts (0) 1	Cleland 85, Negri 39, 40 / Cameron 87	5	0
16/8/97	Celtic (1) 1 / Dunfermline (0) 2	Thom 40 pen / Bingham 46, French 76 pen	7	0
16/8/97	Hearts (3) 4 / Aberdeen (1) 1	Cameron 42, Flogel 89, Fulton 38, Robertson 36 pen / Newell 12	4	1
16/8/97	Motherwell (0) 0 / St Johnstone (0) 1	Grant 65	7	0
17/8/97	Dundee Utd (1) 1 / Hibernian (0) 1	Winters 22 / Tosh 77	4	1
23/8/97	Aberdeen (1) 1 / Motherwell (2) 3	Rowson 26 / Coyne 29, Weir 9, 55	2	0
23/8/97	Dunfermline (0) 2 / Hearts (0) 1	Smith 57, Tod 68 / Hamilton 90	0	0
23/8/97	Hibernian (2) 4 / Kilmarnock (0) 0	Baker 64 og, Crawford 6, Lavety 24, McGinlay 90	2	1
23/8/97	Rangers (3) 5 / Dundee Utd (0) 1	Negri 35, 43, 44, 66, 86 / Pressley 68 pen	4	0
23/8/97	St Johnstone (0) 0 / Celtic (1) 2	Jackson 64, Larsson 45	4	0
30/8/97	Aberdeen (1) 1 / Dundee Utd (1) 1	Dodds 44 / Winters 33	3	0
30/8/97	Dunfermline (1) 2 / St Johnstone (0) 2	Tod 7, 77 / French 68 og, O'Boyle 80	5	0
30/8/97	Hibernian (0) 0 / Hearts (1) 1	McCann 7	2	0
13/9/97	Dundee Utd (0) 1 / Kilmarnock (1) 2	Olofsson 63 / Wright 15, 53 pen	2	0
13/9/97	Hibernian (3) 5 / Dunfermline (1) 2	Charnley 25, 79, Crawford 38, Lavety 31, McGinlay 55 / Millar 16 pen, Petrie 80	4	0
13/9/97	Motherwell (1) 2 / Celtic (0) 3	Coyne 4, 59 / Burley 57, 75, Donnelly 81	8	0
13/9/97	Rangers (1) 3 / Aberdeen (0) 3	Albertz 55, Laudrup 76, Negri 44 pen / Dodds 64, Inglis 78, Newell 58	0	0
13/9/97	St Johnstone (0) 1 / Hearts (1) 2	Tosh 70 / Hamilton 19, 65	3	0
20/9/97	Celtic (2) 2 / Aberdeen (0) 0	Larsson 26, 38	2	0
20/9/97	Hearts (1) 2 / Dundee Utd (1) 1	Pressley 44 og, Robertson 60 / Olofsson 45	2	0
20/9/97	Motherwell (0) 1 / Hibernian (0) 1	Coyne 80 / Rougier 46	3	0
20/9/97	St Johnstone (0) 0 / Rangers (1) 2	Negri 7, 47	0	0
21/9/97	Dunfermline (0) 1 / Kilmarnock (0) 1	Smith 62 / Wright 89 pen	5	0
24/9/97	Kilmarnock (0) 0 / Rangers (0) 3	Negri 49, 62, Stensaas 90	0	0
27/9/97	Aberdeen (1) 1 / Dunfermline (1) 2	Dodds 40 / Bingham 14, Britton 84	4	0
27/9/97	Dundee Utd (0) 1 / Celtic (2) 2	Olofsson 61 / Donnelly 29, O'Donnell 43	5	0
27/9/97	Hibernian (1) 1 / St Johnstone (1) 1	Crawford 2 / Farquhar 16	4	0
27/9/97	Kilmarnock (0) 0 / Hearts (3) 3	Adam 43, Hamilton 14, Weir 6	3	0
27/9/97	Rangers (1) 2 / Motherwell (2) 2	Negri 17, Porrini 63 / Coyne 7, Shivute 44	8	0
4/10/97	Celtic (4) 4 / Kilmarnock (0) 0	Donnelly 33, Larsson 18, 38, Wieghorst 35	0	0
4/10/97	Dunfermline (0) 3 / Dundee Utd (3) 3	Bingham 80, French 69, Smith 64 / McLaren 45, Winters 7, 42	2	1
4/10/97	Hibernian (2) 3 / Rangers (1) 4	Crawford 46, Lavety 43, McGinlay 28 / Albertz 52, Gascoigne 51, Negri 26 pen, 58	1	0
4/10/97	Motherwell (1) 1 / Hearts (3) 4	Coyne 44 pen / Adam 13, Cameron 6, Hamilton 71, McCann 20	0	0
4/10/97	St Johnstone (1) 1 / Aberdeen (0) 0	O'Neil 11	2	0
8/10/97	Kilmarnock (2) 2 / Motherwell (1) 1	Burke 37, Vareille 31 / Shivute 1?	1	0
18/10/97	Aberdeen (2) 2 / Hibernian (0) 0	Dodds 37 pen, Glass 5	6	0
18/10/97	Dundee Utd (2) 4 / Motherwell (0) 0	McLaren 87, McSwegan 77, Olofsson 2, Winters 14	3	0
18/10/97	Hearts (0) 1 / Celtic (2) 2	Cameron 65 / Larsson 21, Rieper 15	7	0
18/10/97	Kilmarnock (0) 0 / St Johnstone (1) 1	O'Halloran 13	2	0
18/10/97	Rangers (3) 7 / Dunfermline (0) 0	Gascoigne 54, 83, Laudrup 16, Negri 21, 34, 80, 88	2	0
25/10/97	Celtic (2) 2 / St Johnstone (0) 0	Donnelly 34 pen, Larsson 31	2	0
25/10/97	Dundee Utd (1) 2 / Rangers (0) 1	Pressley 72 pen, Winters 16 / Negri 59	4	0
25/10/97	Kilmarnock (0) 2 / Hibernian (0) 1	Nevin 57, Roberts 54 / Larusson 80	8	2
25/10/97	Motherwell (0) 1 / Aberdeen (1) 2	Davies 62 / Windass 8, 89	3	0
29/10/97	Hearts (1) 3 / Dunfermline (0) 1	Adam 73, Fulton 90, McCann 13 / Smith 76	3	0
1/11/97	Aberdeen (1) 1 / Hearts (0) 4	Windass 22 / Flogel 65, 82, McCann 54, Smith 76 og	4	0
1/11/97	Dunfermline (0) 0 / Celtic (0) 2	Blinker 67, Larsson 86	5	0
1/11/97	Hibernian (0) 1 / Dundee Utd (1) 3	Crawford 85 / McSwegan 90, Olofsson 26, 88	2	0

Date	Teams & Scores	Goalscorers	Booked	Sent off
1/11/97	Rangers (1) 4 / Kilmarnock (1) 1	Negri 5, 87 pen, 90, Porrini 85 / Mitchell 43	6	0
1/11/97	St Johnstone (2) 4 / Motherwell (0) 3	Grant 49 pen, Kernaghan 18, O'Neil 33, 60 / Coyle 72, Davies 66, Hendry 61 pen	4	0
8/11/97	Hearts (1) 2 / Hibernian (0) 0	Quitongo 88, Robertson 17	3	0
8/11/97	Motherwell (0) 0 / Kilmarnock (0) 1	Roberts 67 pen	5	0
8/11/97	Rangers (1) 1 / Celtic (0) 0	Gough 2	8	0
8/11/97	St Johnstone (0) 0 / Dunfermline (1) 2	Bingham 82, Smith 8	2	0
9/11/97	Dundee Utd (3) 5 / Aberdeen (0) 0	Easton 87, McLaren 21, Olofsson 17, 83, Zetterlund 18	3	0
15/11/97	Aberdeen (1) 1 / Rangers (0) 1	Jess 45 / Albertz 50	6	0
15/11/97	Celtic (0) 0 / Motherwell (1) 2	Coyle 28, Weir 90	8	1
15/11/97	Dunfermline (1) 2 / Hibernian (0) 1	Smith 17, 81 / Crawford 90	3	0
15/11/97	Hearts (0) 2 / St Johnstone (0) 1	Flogel 48, Cameron 90 pen / O'Boyle 77	8	0
15/11/97	Kilmarnock (1) 1 / Dundee Utd (0) 3	Roberts 9 / Perry 65, McSwegan 77, Olofsson 84	4	0
19/11/97	Celtic (0) 1 / Rangers (0) 1	Stubbs 90 / Negri 71	7	1
22/11/97	Celtic (1) 4 / Dundee Utd (0) 0	Thom 35 pen, Larsson 63, Thom 69	1	0
22/11/97	Dunfermline (0) 1 / Aberdeen (0) 1	Petrie 81 / Dodds 66	1	0
22/11/97	Motherwell (0) 1 / Rangers (1) 1	Coyne 80 / McCoist 20	0	0
23/11/97	Hearts (2) 5 / Kilmarnock (1) 3	Adam 10, McCann 28, Adam 61 70, Quitongo 88 / Nevin 5, Holt 62, Roberts 76 pen	3	0
29/11/97	Hibernian (0) 1 / Motherwell (0) 1	Dods 75 / Coyle 90	2	0
29/11/97	Kilmarnock (2) 2 / Dunfermline (1) 1	Nevin 24, 35 / Smith 39	1	0
29/11/97	Rangers (2) 3 / St Johnstone (1) 2	Gattuso 7, Negri 43, 57 / Preston 44, O'Boyle 72	2	0
6/12/97	Aberdeen (0) 1 / St Johnstone (0) 1	Rowson 49 / Grant 80	4	0
6/12/97	Dundee Utd (0) 0 / Dunfermline (0) 0		3	0
6/12/97	Hearts (1) 2 / Motherwell (0) 0	Cameron 45 pen, Flogel 68	5	0
6/12/97	Kilmarnock (0) 0 / Celtic (0) 0		5	0
7/12/97	Rangers (0) 1 / Hibernian (0) 0	Negri 51	6	0
9/12/97	Aberdeen (0) 0 / Celtic (1) 2	Larsson 41, Jackson 74	2	0
9/12/97	Dundee Utd (0) 0 / Hearts (0) 0		4	0
13/12/97	Celtic (0) 1 / Hearts (0) 0	Burley 80	0	0
13/12/97	Dunfermline (0) 0 / Rangers (0) 0		3	0
13/12/97	Hibernian (1) 2 / Aberdeen (1) 2	Walker 2, 83 / Dodds 43, Jess 68	1	0
13/12/97	Motherwell (0) 1 / Dundee Utd (0) 0	Coyle 52	2	0
13/12/97	St Johnstone (0) 1 / Kilmarnock (0) 1	O'Boyle 79 pen / Mitchell 71	3	0
20/12/97	Celtic (2) 5 / Hibernian (0) 0	Burley 23, Wieghorst 38, McNamara 48, Larsson 64, Burley 90	3	0
20/12/97	Dundee Utd (2) 2 / St Johnstone (0) 1	McLaren 10, Olofsson 27 / Kane 83	5	0
20/12/97	Hearts (1) 2 / Rangers (2) 5	Robertson 17, Hamilton 88 / Durie 6, 34, Negri 69 pen, Albertz 78, Durie 86	8	0
20/12/97	Kilmarnock (1) 1 / Aberdeen (0) 0	Wright 27	2	0
20/12/97	Motherwell (0) 2 / Dunfermline (0) 0	Coyle 61, 69	3	0
27/12/97	Aberdeen (0) 3 / Motherwell (0) 0	Windass 63, Jess 83, 86 pen	2	0
27/12/97	Dunfermline (1) 1 / Hearts (3) 3	Bingham 16 pen / Hamilton 7, Westwater 28 og, Salvatori 33	4	0
27/12/97	Hibernian (0) 0 / Kilmarnock (1) 1	Wright 43	4	0
27/12/97	Rangers (2) 4 / Dundee Utd (1) 1	Laudrup 43, Cleland 44, Negri 82, 90 pen / Olofsson 28	8	0
27/12/97	St Johnstone (0) 1 / Celtic (0) 0	O'Boyle 72	3	0
1/1/98	Hearts (2) 2 / Hibernian (0) 2	Fulton 6, 10 / Walker 51, McGinlay 67	3	0
2/1/98	Celtic (0) 2 / Rangers (0) 0	Burley 66, Lambert 85	5	0
3/1/98	Aberdeen (1) 1 / Dundee Utd (0) 0	Windass 26	4	0
3/1/98	Dunfermline (0) 0 / St Johnstone (1) 1	Barnett 7 og	3	0
3/1/98	Kilmarnock (3) 4 / Motherwell (1) 1	Wright 8, 33, Mitchell 44, Roberts 88 / Coyle 24	4	1
10/1/98	Dundee Utd (1) 1 / Kilmarnock (0) 1	Winters 15 / Reilly 69	3	0
10/1/98	Hibernian (1) 1 / Dunfermline (0) 0	Crawford 36	3	0
10/1/98	Motherwell (0) 1 / Celtic (0) 1	Falconer 55 / Lambert 61	2	0
10/1/98	Rangers (2) 2 / Aberdeen (0) 0	Porrini 9, Laudrup 12	5	0
12/1/98	St Johnstone (0) 2 / Hearts (2) 3	Davidson 48, O'Boyle 63 pen; / Hamilton 29, Naysmith 36, Hamilton 70	4	0

Date	Teams & Scores	Goalscorers	Booked	Sent Off
17/1/98	Hibernian (0) 0 / St Johnstone (0) 1	Grant 83	2	0
17/1/98	Kilmarnock (1) 2 / Hearts (2) 2	Wright 40, Reilly 76 / McCann 6, MacPherson 45 og	4	0
17/1/98	Rangers (1) 1 / Motherwell (0) 0	Cleland 23	5	0
27/1/98	Dundee Utd (1) 1 / Celtic (0) 2	Olofsson 24 / Donnelly 78, Burley 87	5	0
28/1/98	Aberdeen (1) 2 / Dunfermline (0) 0	Jess 6, Smith 60	4	0
31/1/98	Dunfermline (1) 3 / Kilmarnock (1) 2	Barnett 41, Smith 67, Shaw 76 / Vareille 2, Roberts 85	5	0
31/1/98	Hearts (1) 2 / Dundee Utd (0) 0	Cameron 30, 79	0	0
31/1/98	Motherwell (3) 6 / Hibernian (2) 2	Arnott 10, Weir 23, Garcin 43, McCulloch 81, Crawford 4, Lavety 8 \ Coyne 88, McCulloch	4	1
31/1/98	St Johnstone (1) 2 / Rangers (0) 0	O'Neil 36, O'Boyle 69	0	0
1/2/98	Celtic (2) 3 / Aberdeen (1) 1	Wieghorst 21, Larsson 35, Jackson 82 / Rowson 8	3	0
7/2/98	Aberdeen (1) 3 / Hibernian (0) 0	Newell 40, Jess 57, Miller 59	2	0
7/2/98	Dundee Utd (0) 1 / Motherwell (0) 0	Olofsson 68	1	0
7/2/98	Kilmarnock (0) 1 / St Johnstone (0) 0	Reilly 90	3	0
7/2/98	Rangers (0) 1 / Dunfermline (0) 1	Porrini 72 / Curran 90	1	0
8/2/98	Hearts (0) 1 / Celtic (1) 1	Quitongo 89 / McNamara	3	0
21/2/98	Celtic (2) 4 / Kilmarnock (0) 0	Brattbakk 11, 36, 70, 87	3	0
21/2/98	Dunfermline (0) 2 / Dundee Utd (1) 2	Smith 52, 90 / McSwegan 40, 80	0	0
21/2/98	Hibernian (1) 1 / Rangers (1) 2	Lavety 19 / Negri 35, Albertz 88	6	1
21/2/98	Motherwell (2) 2 / Hearts (1) 4	Coyle 6, Falconer 37 / Hamilton 38, 58, Fulton 64, Adam 87	3	0
21/2/98	St Johnstone (0) 0 / Aberdeen (1) 1	Dodds 14	1	0
24/2/98	Dundee Utd (0) 1 / Hibernian (0) 1	Dow 73 og / Hughes 75	1	0
24/2/98	Kilmarnock (1) 1 / Rangers (0) 1	Wright 15 / Thern 68	2	0
25/2/98	Celtic (3) 5 / Dunfermline (0) 1	Larsson 4, Brattbakk 28, 40, O'Donnell 61, Tod 74 \ Wieghorst 68	2	0
25/2/98	Hearts (1) 3 / Aberdeen (0) 1	Hamilton 2, Naysmith 63, McCann 77 / Jess 61	0	0
25/2/98	Motherwell (2) 2 / St Johnstone (0) 1	Coyne 11, 19 / O'Boyle 61 pen	6	0
28/2/98	Aberdeen (0) 0 / Kilmarnock (0) 0		3	1
28/2/98	Hibernian (0) 0 / Celtic (1) 1	Rieper 25	1	0
28/2/98	Rangers (1) 2 / Hearts (1) 2	Albertz 40, 90 / McCann 31, Hamilton 76	7	2
28/2/98	St Johnstone (0) 1 / Dundee Utd (1) 1	Grant 75 / Winters 22	0	0
7/3/98	Dunfermline (1) 2 / Motherwell (1) 1	Smith 23, 61 / Coyne 12	3	0
14/3/98	Dunfermline (0) 3 / Aberdeen (1) 3	Tod 46, 53, Shaw 80 / Rowson 19, 64, O'Neil 70	2	0
14/3/98	Hearts (1) 1 / Kilmarnock (1) 1	McPherson 23 / Henry 34	1	0
14/3/98	Motherwell (1) 2 / Rangers (1) 1	Coyle 44, Falconer 87 / McCoist 12	4	0
14/3/98	St Johnstone (0) 1 / Hibernian (0) 1	McQuillan 62 / Rougier 90 pen	1	0
15/3/98	Celtic (1) 1 / Dundee Utd (0) 1	Donnelly 27 / Olofsson 75	4	0
21/3/98	Aberdeen (0) 0 / Celtic (1) 1	Burley 45 pen	6	0
21/3/98	Dundee Utd (0) 0 / Hearts (1) 1	Hamilton 8	4	1
21/3/98	Hibernian (1) 1 / Motherwell (0) 0	Lavety 34	4	1
21/3/98	Kilmarnock (0) 3 / Dunfermline (0) 0	Wright 62 pen, Nevin 65, McIntyre 69	3	1
21/3/98	Rangers (1) 2 / St Johnstone (1) 1	Negri 27, Thern 56 / Kernaghan 15	2	0
28/3/98	Celtic (0) 0 / Hearts (0) 0		3	0
28/3/98	Dunfermline (1) 2 / Rangers (1) 3	Smith 35, 63 / McCoist 27, 48, Thern 68	1	0
28/3/98	Hibernian (0) 1 / Aberdeen (0) 1	Rougier 90 pen / Jess 68	3	0
28/3/98	Motherwell (0) 1 / Dundee Utd (0) 0	Coyle 52	0	0
28/3/98	St Johnstone (1) 1 / Kilmarnock (0) 0	O'Neil 1	4	0
1/4/98	Rangers (0) 3 / Hibernian (0) 0	McCoist 56, Thern 58, Durie 75	3	0
4/4/98	Aberdeen (0) 0 / St Johnstone (1) 1	O'Boyle 19	1	0
7/4/98	Dundee Utd (0) 2 / Dunfermline (2) 2	Olofsson 48, Malpas 70 / Millar 19, Britton 25	0	0
8/4/98	Hearts (0) 1 / Motherwell (0) 1	McCann 59 / Coyne 79	4	0
8/4/98	Kilmarnock (1) 1 / Celtic (1) 2	Burke 40 / Larsson 19, Donnelly 55	1	0
11/4/98	Dundee Utd (0) 0 / Aberdeen (0) 0		4	0
11/4/98	Hibernian (0) 2 / Hearts (0) 1	Lavety 56, Harper 80 / Robertson 71	5	0

Every game of the season

Date	Teams & Scores		Goalscorers	Booked	Sent off
11/4/98	Motherwell	(0) 1	Lindqvist 80	0	
	Kilmarnock	(1) 1	Holt 28	0	
11/4/98	St Johnstone	(0) 0		2	
	Dunfermline	(0) 0		0	
12/4/98	Rangers	(1) 2	Thern 24, Albertz 66	6	
	Celtic	(0) 0		0	
18/4/98	Celtic	(2) 4	Burley 25, 43, Donnelly 49, 62	1	
	Motherwell	(1) 1	McMillan 12	0	
18/4/98	Dunfermline	(0) 1	Brebner 48 og	7	
	Hibernian	(0) 1	Welsh 90	0	
18/4/98	Hearts	(0) 1	McPherson 75	2	
	St Johnstone	(0) 1	Grant 78	0	
18/4/98	Kilmarnock	(1) 1	Burke 2	1	
	Dundee Utd	(0) 0		0	
19/4/98	Aberdeen	(1) 1	Glass 28	7	
	Rangers	(0) 0		1	
25/4/98	Celtic	(0) 0		4	
	Hibernian	(0) 0		0	
25/4/98	Dundee Utd	(0) 0		2	
	St Johnstone	(0) 2	Jenkinson 66, O'Boyle 89	1	
25/4/98	Hearts	(0) 0		0	
	Rangers	(0) 3	Gattuso 48, Albertz 65, Gattuso 78	1	
25/4/98	Kilmarnock	(1) 2	Vareille 33, 85	4	
	Aberdeen	(1) 1	Dodds 44	0	
25/4/98	Motherwell	(1) 1	Shivute 28	4	
	Dunfermline	(2) 3	Smith 18, Ireland 31, Britton 54	0	
2/5/98	Aberdeen	(1) 2	Jess 26, Newell 4	2	
	Hearts	(2) 2	McCann 10, McPherson 29	0	
2/5/98	Hibernian	(1) 1	Brebner 31	2	
	Dundee Utd	(0) 2	Olofsson 72, 78	0	
2/5/98	Rangers	(0) 0		1	
	Kilmarnock	(0) 1	Mitchell 90	0	
2/5/98	St Johnstone	(1) 3	Jenkinson 15, 88, McCluskey 70	3	
	Motherwell	(1) 2	Martin 4, Coyle 58 pen	0	
3/5/98	Dunfermline	(0) 1	Faulconbridge 83	0	
	Celtic	(1) 1	Donnelly 35	0	
9/5/98	Celtic	(1) 2	Larsson 3, Brattbakk 72	0	
	St Johnstone	(0) 1		0	
9/5/98	Dundee Utd	(0) 1	Olofsson	0	
	Rangers	(1) 2	Laudrup 31, Albertz 53 pen	1	
9/5/98	Hearts	(1) 2	Adam 22, Holmes 82	0	
	Dunfermline	(0) 0		0	
9/5/98	Kilmarnock	(1) 1	Roberts 15	0	
	Hibernian	(0) 1	Crawford 89	0	
9/5/98	Motherwell	(0) 1	Ross 66	2	
	Aberdeen	(2) 2	Dodds 1 pen 22	0	

Allsport

Action Images

August

Premiership 1997

The start of the season and anything seems possible. Although Ranger's tenth successive title looks more possible than most things.

Celtic get off to a terrible start. Back to back defeats by Hibernian and Dunfermline leave supporters rueing the loss of **Paolo di Canio** and **Jorge Cadete**. Celtic look bereft of flair or inspiration in attack. Paolo defies orders by general manager **Jock Brown** to return to Celtic park. To avoid massive embarrassment they eventually trade him with Sheffield Wednesday for Dutch star **Regi Blinker**. **Cadete** is rumoured to be suffering from woman trouble and the consequent psychological backlash means he is no longer seen at the hallowed Parkhead turf. And to cap it all, the appointment of new coach **Wim Jansen** is treated with derision by the fans.

Meanwhile, potential pretenders to the title, Hearts, are compelled to endure the unveiling of the Championship flag at Ibrox. They are given a roasting by the reigning champions. **Marco Negri** scores a controversial first Scottish Premier league goal and is so taken aback at how easy it is, he does it again sixty seconds later. He further cements his embryonic divine status by scoring all five goals in the destruction of previous Rangers bugbears, Dundee United. The goals equal the Premier League record held by Paul Sturrock when he put five past Morton in 1984.

LEAGUE POSITIONS

HIBERNIAN	4	7
DUNFERMLINE	4	7
RANGERS	2	6
MOTHERWELL	3	6
HEARTS	4	6
ST JOHNSTONE	4	5
CELTIC	3	3
DUNDEE	4	3
ABERDEEN	4	2
KILMARNOCK	2	1

As if to make up for the Old Firm stumbling block, Hearts assert themselves in their first home match against Aberdeen. **Roy Aitken**'s duffers are defeated at Tynecastle for the first time since October 1994. Another Hearts hoodoo is also broken in this match – the final score of 4–1 is the highest Premier league victory recorded by Hearts over the Pittodrie pushovers. The elation doesn't last for long though. High-flying Dunfermline run the visiting capital city men ragged in the type of match which the Pars are famous for – spirited, physical, route one football. Despite the defeat, Hearts' **Neil McCann** puts on a running show which encourages the Tynecastle faithful for the future.

New kids on the block, St Johnstone, get off to a solid, if uninspired start, recording draws against Dundee United and Dunfermline and a victory against potential relegation strugglers Motherwell. Unfortunately for them, their defeat against Celtic lights the Glasgow team's touch paper for a run of eight straight league victories.

The biggest surprise of the month belongs to the performance of Hearts Edinburgh rivals, Hibernian. Having narrowly avoided relegation in the play-offs the previous season, they sit atop the league at the end of August. Their endeavours owe much to the inspirational midfield play of wayward star **Chic Charnley**. Claims of 'Charnley for Scotland' are treated seriously by the media and even more seriously by Hibernian's fans. A historically inevitable defeat from their Edinburgh derby rivals at Tynecastle does little to dampen the Easter Road men's new found enthusiasm for the game.

TOP GOALSCORERS

7	Negri
3	Coyne, Tod
2	Winters
1	Smith, Newell, Thorn, Dodds, French, Jackson, Lavety

Wayward Chic Charnley may be considered for Scotland.

September

Premiership 1997

Autumn draws on and the season really gets under way with convincing performances marching the Edinburgh teams to the top.

Hibernian consolidate their unlikely Premier Division lead with a convincing 5-2 rout of Dunfermline. **Chic Charnley** is once again the orchestrator of the team and caps his performance by bagging a double. It is the last time he scores for the Hibees and it is the last victory for Hibernian in 1997.

The inevitable happens and Hearts leapfrog their capital rivals the following week. A less than convincing win against Dundee United is only their second home game of the season and the first in front of their newly completed stand. Tynecastle's capacity now exceeds 18,000.

Aberdeen begin to show signs of being able to play as a cohesive unit. Their hard fought match against Rangers at Ibrox ends in a creditable 3-3 draw. But it is a false dawn. The next two matches see them crash and burn at Celtic Park and lose at home to Dunfermline despite the Fifers being reduced to ten men for the last half hour of the match. Serious questions are being asked over the future tenure of **Roy Aitken** at Pittodrie. The only light in an otherwise tawdry season is their Coca-Cola cup performance. Stirling Albion are dismissed and Aberdeen claim their right to a place in the semi-final.

LEAGUE POSITIONS

HEARTS	5	15
RANGERS	6	14
HIBERNIAN	7	2
CELTIC	6	12
DUNFERMLINE	7	11
MOTHERWELL	6	8
ST JOHNSTONE	7	6
KILMARNOCK	6	5
DUNDEE	7	3
ABERDEEN	7	3

More worrying for Rangers is their performance against the Dons. **Negri** scores, as ever, but the team begin showing shortcomings in defence and Laudrup is failing to deliver his particular form of magic. It does not bode well for the up and coming UEFA Cup fixture at Strasbourg. They lose 2–1 and in the return leg at Ibrox a fortnight later, they again drag the name of Scottish football through the European mud by losing 2–1 on home turf. Strasbourg have one of the poorest records in the French First Division.

Marc Rieper, Celtic's new £1.5 million signing from West Ham makes his debut against Aberdeen. The Danish international defender contributes to a stylish performance and ensures that the second league shutout of Celtic's season isn't going to be their last.

Celtic fare better in Europe than their Glasgow counterparts. Unlike Rangers, there are no raised expectations for the visit of Liverpool to Parkhead. Pundits expect the alleged superiority of the English team to be too much for the mostly non-Scottish Celtic to handle. The UEFA match is a thrilling encounter which ends in a creditable 2–2 draw. No goals appear in the return leg and Celtic go out of the competition unbeaten.

In the European Cup Winners' Cup, Kilmarnock are soundly beaten by a distinctly average Nice. The result is compounded by the fact that Nice play in the French Second division and are performing poorly.

The month finishes in the pattern that the league will follow over the coming months; Hearts on top, Rangers one point behind with a game in hand, Celtic three points behind with a game in hand. Hearts supporters, unlike everyone else, begin to believe.

TOP GOALSCORERS

13	Negri
7	Coyne
2	Olofsson, Hamilton
3	Winters, Donnelly, Smith, Newell
1	Thom

Aberdeen, whose performance had improved enough to hold Rangers to a 3–3 draw, crashed at Celtic Park and then they lost at home to Dunfermline.

Winning their match against Dundee on 20th September put Hearts at the top of the table

October

Premiership 1997

The eventual winner of the league is anyone's guess as three teams take it in turns at the top, but Rangers are beginning to show form...

The top three begin playing musical chairs with their league positioning. Hearts hold onto the top spot for the first week of October. The Old Firm hold a game in hand up their sleeves. Before trying to convert the potential advantage, Celtic face Hearts at the capital city men's home ground. It is only Hearts' third home tie and, aping the result against Rangers, they lose. **Marc Rieper** scores his first goal for the Bhoys. Complemented by the indefatigable **Larsson** it is enough for the Hoops to take all three points back to Glasgow.

The implication of Hearts losing at home twice in the first quarter to the Old Firm isn't lost on the media. Hearts' fine start to the season is written off as the spice on the meat of the real title challenge between the two Glasgow clubs. Hearts are expected to falter from here on in.

The arrival of **Richard Gough** to bolster a shaky Rangers defence is eclipsed by the performance of **Paul Gascoigne** against Dunfermline. He orchestrates a crushing 7–0 blow to the Fifers' survival hopes. It's vintage Gascoigne as he makes and takes goals. He sets up two for **Negri** but reserves the best two of the match for himself. Speculation that the wayward geordie may be leaving is laid to rest for the

LEAGUE POSITIONS		
CELTIC	9	21
HEARTS	10	21
RANGERS	9	20
HIBERNIAN	10	12
ST JOHNSTONE	10	12
DUNFERMLINE	10	12
KILMARNOCK	10	11
DUNDEE	10	10
ABERDEEN	10	9
MOTHERWELL	10	8

time being. On this form, Rangers fans can already see their hallowed ten in a row in the distance. The result takes the Gers to the top of the table.

The ascendancy is short lived however. Dundee United, mirroring the impressive form shown in the previous season, topple Rangers. The blame is laid firmly at the door of **Andy Goram**. In previous seasons his footwork with backpasses was immaculate. This time, he tries to side-step the impressive **Robbie Winters**. Winters easily steals the ball off of the ailing international and rolls the ball calmly into the net. "It is the first time since the back pass rule came in that I've seen Andy struggle." comments **Walter Smith** after the game. It isn't the last time that mistakes like this by Goram will cost Rangers a goal and a result.

Capitalising on Goram's misery,

Celtic take their turn at the top. St Johnstone's occasional lapses of collective concentration allow **Wim Jansen**'s men to punish their mistakes and put on a show of silky soccer to the delight of the 50,000 sell-out home crowd.

Meanwhile Aberdeen finally manage to wrest themselves from the bottom of the table. A gritty, if undeserved, victory over the Steelmen of Motherwell consigns their hapless opponents to the relegation zone. **Roy Aitken** breathes a sigh of relief as he believes the Dons have finally turned the corner.

TOP GOALSCORERS	
20	Negri
8	Coyne
7	Larsson
6	Winters
5	Hamilton, Olofsson
4	Donnelly, Dodds, Cameron, Crawford
3	Smith, Wright, Lavety, Charnley
2	Newell, Burley
1	McSwegan, Thom
6	Winters

Rangers destroyed Dunfermline 7–0, while goalscoring Dean Windlass helped Aberdeen off the bottom of the table against Motherwell.

November
Premiership 1997

The pitches start getting hard and so does life at the top as both Edinburgh and Glasgow derbies dominate the league.

Bonfire month lay host to some of the most intense fireworks displays in the Premier league so far. The Old Firm meet at Ibrox for their first league encounter of the season. Celtic come into the fixture sporting an impressive run of eight straight league victories behind them. A stodgy-sounding 1–0 victory to the Gers, belies a complete trouncing of the supposedly rejuvenated Celtic. In keeping with these ill-tempered affairs, a rash of yellow cards from both sides eventually results in the sending off of Frenchman **Stephen Mahe** for one too many zealous tackles on the illustrious **Laudrup**. Celtic's fans are unable to believe the timidity of **Wim Jansen**'s tactics. **Gascoigne**, **Thern** and **Laudrup** are almost allowed free rein in midfield.

Paul Lambert, transferred from Borussia Dortmund earlier in the week, comes on as a late substitute in the second half. He finds himself frantically trying to plug the huge holes in defence due to the dismissal of **Mahe**. On this evidence, **Jansen** is forced to rethink his Old Firm strategy.

Capitalising on the craven showing of the Bhoys, Hearts record their 100th league victory over their derby rivals, Hibernian. **John Robertson**, playing his 501st game for the Jambos, scores

LEAGUE POSITIONS		
HEARTS	14	33
RANGERS	14	29
CELTIC	14	28
DUNDEE	14	19
DUNFERMLINE	14	19
ST JOHNSTONE	14	18
KILMARNOCK	14	14
HIBERNIAN	14	12
MOTHERWELL	14	12
ABERDEEN	14	11

the first goal. It is his 25th goal against the Hibees and his 268th in his playing career at Hearts. Hibernian are faced with the stark fact that they've failed to record a goal against Hearts in their previous five outings. Robertson's substitution in the 69th minute receives a standing ovation from the Tynecastle faithful. The 2–0 victory again places Hearts at the top of the table. It is a position they will hold for the rest of the month.

After the excitement of the Edinburgh and Glasgow derbies has died down, drama of a different kind unfolds the next day on live terrestrial television. Dundee United humiliate Aberdeen. A devastating four-minute period in the first half sees a trio of well worked goals kill the visitors off. Another two in the second completes the demolition. Historic embarrassment

Photo News Scotland

is avoided due to a heroic showing by **Jim Leighton** in goal. **Roy Aitken**, to the relief of Aberdeen's fans, is sacked the next day.

The second Old Firm meeting of the

9th November – Dundee United 5 Aberdeen 0: Without doubt the most sorrowful episode in a tale of woe for a once-proud club. Despite possessing one of the strongest squads on paper, Aberdeen cave in to a rampant United. The board have no option other than showing Aitken the door.

An Ill-tempered affair: A rash of yellow cards for both Rangers and Celtic results in Stephen Mahe being sent off.

TOP GOALSCORERS

26	Negri
10	Larsson, Olofsson
9	Coyne
8	Smith
6	Winters, Adam
5	Dodds, McCann
4	Donnelly
3	Thom, McSwegan, Wright
1	McCoist, Coyle

month and the second of the season is played in a midweek tie at Parkhead. Like it's predecessor yellow cards are shown in abundance. **Paul Gascoigne** lifts his hands to **Morten Wieghorst**

and receives his first sending off in Scottish domestic competition. Despite the ten man disadvantage, **Negri** opens the scoring for Rangers. It looks like the playing out of a familiar script until a sensational injury time strike from **Alan Stubbs** leaves the game all square. Tellingly, it is the first goal Celtic have scored against the Gers at Celtic Park for four years.

December

Premiership 1997

The festive season sees the Old Firm close in on the lead, but Hearts refuse to lie down for them.

Hearts face the stiffest test of their championship challenging credentials yet. And fail. Miserably. Two consecutive fixtures against the Old Firm result in two consecutive defeats. The first, against Celtic at Celtic Park, is a tense and fraught affair. Encouragingly, Hearts aren't outplayed the way they were the last time the two met. But they rarely look capable of scoring either. **Harald Brattbakk**, Celtic's new £2 million signing from Rosenborg, makes his debut with half an hour to go. There's to be no fairy tale introduction for the Scandinavian. **Craig Burley** wraps the fixture up with his own particular brand of mid-field class and the only goal of the match.

Despite the setback, Hearts remain at the top of the table. Rangers have unbelievably been held to a no-score draw at Dunfermline's East End Park.

However, the respite for Hearts is only temporary. The visit of the reigning Champions teaches the Jambos a sharp lesson in the psychology of football. The home fans have to endure a dispiriting demolition of their title-chasing favourites and then have to further endure the reverberations of the media writing their title aspirations off.

The 5–2 defeat is a crushing blow, especially at home. Rangers are superior in every department of play.

LEAGUE POSITIONS		
RANGERS	19	42
HEARTS	19	40
CELTIC	19	38
KILMARNOCK	19	25
DUNDEE	19	24
ST JOHNSTONE	19	23
DUNFERMLINE	19	21
MOTHERWELL	19	19
ABERDEEN	19	16
HIBERNIAN	19	14

On this evidence, **Jim Jefferies'** claim that Hearts could lose every game against the Old Firm and still win the title sounds hollow.

The win puts Rangers back at the top. One point clear of Celtic who, facing the other Edinburgh side, dish out a defeat as comprehensive as it is workmanlike. Hibernian are stripped and sanded of any footballing veneer they may have possessed before this visit to Celtic's home. It was Hibernian's last chance of recording an away win in 1997. The 5–0 scoreline served as a summary of their away form for the year.

Hearts' next match after the Rangers' hiding is a supreme test of character. They pass with flying colours. Dunfermline are outplayed through guile and flair in equal measure. **Stefano Salvatori** scores his first league goal for Hearts and it's one of those straight out of Serie A 25-yard net-buster.

The Jambos' win moves them into second place. Celtic fall victim to the least praised but most organised team in the league – St Johnstone. The victory signals a continuing drive of upward mobility for the Perthshire men. Their West coast rivals, Kilmarnock continue their relentless surge toward fourth spot, finally claiming it in the last match of the year against Hibernian at Easter Road. The 1–0 victory becomes Killie's fifth consecutive match without defeat. The new year can't come soon enough.

TOP GOALSCORERS	
30	Negri
12	Larsson, Olofsson
9	Coyne
8	Smith
7	Hamilton
6	Winters, Dodds, Coyle, Adam
5	Burley, Wright
4	Donnelly
3	McSwegan

Against Hearts, Harald Brattbakk, Celtic's new £2 million signing, makes his debut but leaves Craig Burley to wrap up with the only goal of the match.

Gordon Durie completes his hat-trick in the 5–2 victory over Hearts

January

Premiership 1998

The New Year comes, but it doesn't look any clearer at the top with three teams absolutely neck and neck.

January brings a green and white reversal of fortune in an ominous throw of the runes for the Bhoys. Rangers are comprehensively beaten at Celtic Park by a 2–0 scoreline which flatters them. They are comprehensively outclassed. The result is Celtic's first league win over Rangers in 11 matches and their first in the New Year derby since 1988 – their centenary season and the last time they won a championship.

The Gers' lead is cut to one point leaving Hearts to rue the 2–0 half-time lead they held over city rivals Hibernian. A lax second half performance lets the relegation favourites back into the match. Hibs wrest a creditable draw after being geed up by a half-time pep talk which leaves manager **Jim Duffy** fighting to regain his voice. West Coast cynics point out that all four goals in the draw were scored by Old firm cast-offs. All **Jim Jefferies** cares about are the two carelessly dropped points – their capture would have put Hearts back on top.

Unable to capitalise on the psychological boost of the new year derby, Celtic's next match at Fir Park is a game rich in heroes and villains. Finding themselves 1–0 down and unable to penetrate a resolute Motherwell defence, **Paul Lambert**

LEAGUE POSITIONS		
RANGERS	23	48
CELTIC	23	48
HEARTS	23	48
ST JOHNSTONE	23	32
KILMARNOCK	23	30
DUNDEE	23	25
DUNFERMLINE	23	24
MOTHERWELL	23	23
ABERDEEN	23	22
HIBERNIAN	23	18

drives a 35-yard shot into the Well's net with blistering audacity. Gaining the momentary upper hand, Celtic win a penalty ten minutes later after the assistant referee spots **Brian Martin** pull **Larsson** down in the box. Career substitute and Scotland international **Darren Jackson** screws the resulting penalty too far to the left and helps Celtic unnecessarily draw instead of win.

Back at mighty Ibrox, Rangers put on a show of football which has been mostly absent the whole season. Aberdeen are the victims and they are made to look like rank amateurs. Only Leighton in goal keeps the score respectable at 2–0. In every other way it is a lesson in humiliation and superiority.

The last day of January ends in high drama – Rangers are beaten for the first time in 27 years by St Johnstone.

It's no fluke. A poor Rangers are outmanoeuvred and outplayed – and they deserve to lose. The result lets Celtic make up the point difference between the teams and lets St Johnstone leapfrog Kilmarnock for fourth. Only goal difference keeps the Champions on top.

As if to cap another tumultuous month, **Jim Duffy** is sacked. In an unbelievable change of fortune, Hibernian take a quick 2–0 lead against Motherwell at Fir Park. In keeping with their inability to win away from home, they relinquish the lead and then succumb to a rampant Well. The final score of 6–2, and how it was achieved, feels like a cruel metaphor of the Hibernian season so far.

TOP GOALSCORERS	
30	Negri
13	Olofsson
12	Larsson
10	Coyne
9	Smith, Hamilton
8	Wright, Cameron, Crawford
7	Winters, Burley, Coyle, O'Boyle
5	Donnelly
3	McSwegan

Allsport

Photo News Scotland

The Bhoys think there may be something in this American football strategy thing after alL...

February

Premiership 1998

As Valentine's Day comes into sight there are three teams still left in the race for the title. Surely three's a crowd...?

Hearts show character and psychological strength in every match of this testing month. Outplayed at home by Celtic, they never crumble and never give up. Unable to capitalise on a first half **Burley** goal, Celtic set up enough chances to win the game four times over. Fingers are pointed at the inability of **Harald Brattbakk** to convert the numerous chances that come his way. The criticism reaches boiling point when, close on the stroke of full time, substitute **Jose Quitongo** sneaks an equaliser against the rampant Celts.

After the match **Wim Jansen** defends Brattbakk's hapless performance, "The important thing is that he was in the right place to make the chance. If he keeps doing that, the goals will come."

And come they did. Against Kilmarnock at Celtic Park. The dispirited Ayrshiremen are dissembled and dissolved by a classy Celtic showing. **Braatbakk** scores all four goals and manages to miss four sitters. It is the first time he scores in a league game since joining Celtic. The last Celtic player to score four goals in a match was **Frank MacAvennie** in 1987. The real hero of the Brattbakk carnival though is **Larsson**. His intelligence and speed of thought makes the goals and

breaks the Kilmarnock defence.

In contrast to the surging confidence of the Celts, Rangers struggle throughout the month. Their only victory, against Hibs, is unconvincing. The only light being the continuous increase in form of wayward German star **Jorg Albertz**. His thundering left foot salvages a point against Hearts and all three from Hibernian.

The season's injury list at Ibrox is compounded when in a sickening clash of heads with Kilmarnock's **Gary Holt**, **Gordon Durie** is stretchered off unconcious. It takes a full month before the Scotland international is fit to play again. The incident overshadows **Paul Wright**'s 100th Premier League goal. He is the thirteenth player since the inception of that league to reach such a heady height.

Brattbakk's next match after his goal scoring extravaganza against Killie sees him add to his tally in a five goal decimation of the Pars. This time he only gets a pair, but his finishing bodes well for the league run in. In the same match, **Morten Wieghorst** scores one of the best goals seen all season. It is the icing on the cake of Celtic's rise up the table.

LEAGUE POSITIONS		
CELTIC	27	58
HEARTS	27	56
RANGERS	27	54
KILMARNOCK	27	35
ST JOHNSTONE	27	33
DUNDEE	27	31
ABERDEEN	27	29
DUNFERMLINE	27	29
MOTHERWELL	27	26
HIBERNIAN	27	19

TOP GOALSCORERS	
31	Negri
14	Larsson, Olofsson
13	Hamilton
12	Coyne
11	Smith
9	Wright
8	Winters, Coyle, O'Boyle, McCann
7	Albertz, Burley
6	Brattbakk
5	McSwegan, Donnelly

Jim Hamilton celebrates at Ibrox on 28th February as he puts Hearts 2–1 to Rangers in the 76th minute, only to have Albertz equalise at the last minute.

Henrik Larsson gets off to a fast start with a goal at only four minutes in the 5–1 match against Dunfermline on 25th February.

March

Premiership 1998

Only a few games left to go and the title race is still wide open. Will Rangers get their record? Or can Celtic continue to thwart them?

Fever pitch. The excitement of the title run in is accentuated by mistakes on the field and punctuated by drama off it. **Gascoigne** plays in his last match for Rangers before being bundled off to Division One promotion hopefuls Middlesbrough. The Rangers fans are livid and fear the worst. An insipid and spiritless Gers are rejuvenated by the committed passion of venerable veteran and World Cup hopeful **Ally McCoist**. Despite this newly discovered passion, the Bluenoses still manage to falter and fail against the Steelmen of Motherwell.

Coisty, on only his second league start of the season, scores the first goal. He's unlucky not to make it a hat-trick. The woodwork denies him twice. Motherwell, as so often before, become the bane of the Old Firm yet again. Evergreen striker **Tommy Coyne** gives the Well the psychological edge by equalising on the verge of half time. This edge is converted into victory by the hawking skills of **Willie Falconer**. His heroic heading dive delivers a much needed win and virtually ensures Premier league football for next season.

Hearts, meanwhile, are lucky to escape with a draw against a Kilmarnock side with an agenda all their own. The Tynecastle crowd are treated to a scintillating match of

LEAGUE POSITIONS		
CELTIC	30	63
HEARTS	30	61
RANGERS	30	60
KILMARNOCK	30	39
ST JOHNSTONE	30	37
DUNDEE	30	32
MOTHERWELL	30	32
ABERDEEN	27	29
DUNFERMLINE	30	30
HIBERNIAN	30	24

non-stop end-to-end attacking football. The ascendancy belongs to Kilmarnock but they cannot capitalise on their undoubted superiority. **Jim Jefferies** admits that the result isn't so much two points dropped as a point gained.

Both results mean that Celtic, playing Dundee United on the Sunday, can open a four-point gap on Hearts and seven on Rangers. They bottle it in front of a capacity home crowd and a live television audience. Despite having beaten the Tangerine Terrors five times already in the season, they meekly acquiesce toward a draw. United are spared the embarrassment of a league whitewash and both the other title challengers can breathe to fight again.

Rangers capitalise on another draw at Celtic Park. This time the match concerns Hearts. Despite **Neil McCann**'s show of form against

the Bhoys, it isn't enough for the Edinburgh men to gain a victory. Celtic never look like scoring either. The match is exciting, but the only net gain is achieved by Rangers in a hard fought match against the hard men of Fife, Dunfermline. Celtic still retain their top spot, but the potentially huge gap between them and the others has been reduced by their jittery run.

McCoist returns: the veteran Rangers and international player (here playing for Scotland against Austria at the end of September) rejuvenates the side.

Neil McCann shows his form, but it isn't enough for the Edinburgh men to gain a victory over Celtic.

TOP GOALSCORERS	
32	Negri
15	Smith, Olofsson
14	Larsson, Hamilton
13	Coyne
10	Coyle, Wright
8	Winters, Burley, O'Boyle
7	Albertz
6	Donnelly
5	McSwegan
4	McCoist

April

Premiership 1998

Everyone has something to play for, but for Celtic, a rare home defeat of Kilmarnock puts them in with a chance to break Rangers' nine-year run.

April proves to be as turbulent in the league as the weather afflicting Scotland. No matches are meaningless. Every team has something to play for, whether that be the title, a European spot, or merely to save themselves from the fiscal disaster of relegation.

Hearts' bubble finally bursts. Throughout April they fail to record a single victory and lose twice. Their play in their opening midweek match against Motherwell at Tynecastle seems to lose its vigour. Despite holding a half-time lead, the Well conjure up another gritty performance and **Tommy Coyne** delivers the first of the knockout blows which eventually flatten the Jambo challenge.

While Coyne was damaging Hearts, Celtic lay to rest another of the bugbears which have haunted their league aspirations in the past. Kilmarnock are barely beaten at Rugby Park. It is the first time Celtic have managed this since 1996 and is the first home defeat in five months for the Ayrshiremen. The result puts the Bhoys three points clear of Rangers and four ahead of Hearts. It also allows St Johnstone to retain fourth position and a potential UEFA spot over Killie.

Rangers, meanwhile, find that the loss of **Gascoigne** is a blessing in disguise. His contribution to the Gers,

LEAGUE POSITIONS		
CELTIC	34	70
RANGERS	34	69
HEARTS	34	63
KILMARNOCK	34	46
ST JOHNSTONE	34	45
DUNFERMLINE	34	36
ABERDEEN	34	35
DUNDEE	34	34
MOTHERWELL	34	34
HIBERNIAN	34	29

in retrospect, has had the effect of diminishing the performance of Rangers as a coherent team unit. With him gone, responsibility is gladly accepted and lived up to by other members of the squad. For the first time in the league campaign, Rangers continue a run of straight victories which stretches beyond this season's customary two-before-a-falter. The switch in tempo is highlighted when, despite being under the cosh for large swathes of the match, Rangers defeat Celtic. Their resilience and composure is rewarded by one goal each from the increasingly valuable **Jorg Albertz** and **Jonas Thern**. Both players are hitting peak form when it is most needed.

The victory takes Rangers to the top of the table on goal difference. The Bluenose Scottish media establishment have a field day – the chosen might

still make it ten in a row. But they reckon without the contribution from an Aberdeen side who, despite continuing poor form, can never be discounted. Needle has been needlessly added due to barbed comments in Ian Durrant's autobiography. Aberdeen lift their game contain the champions and score in the first half. They hold out and inflict a crucial defeat.

Celtic, having already banked the points against Motherwell stay at the top with a far healthier goal difference. But jitters still appear in the ranks of the hoops. At Celtic Park, the visiting Hibernian show too much fight for the meek champions in waiting. The match results in stalemate with no goals scored. Rangers draw back to within a point with an emphatic win over broken Hearts. May is going to see the most exciting end to a league campaign in years.

TOP GOALSCORERS	
32	Negri
16	Smith, Olofsson
15	Larsson
14	Coyne, Hamilton
10	Burley, Coyle, Wright, O'Boyle
9	Donnelly, Albertz
8	Winters
6	Brattbakk
5	McCoist, McSwegan

Jonas Thern fights it out with Simon Donnelly, while Jorg Albertz keeps ahead of Paul Lambert – both Rangers players on top form when it's most needed on 12th April.

Action Images

LAST DAY OF THE SEASON

Saturday 9th May, 3pm. The last day of the season and an historic day for Scottish Football. Celtic are poised on the verge of their first championship in ten years. They need to win against St Johnstone to ensure that they end Rangers' stranglehold on the title.

Rangers know that if they win against Dundee United, and Celtic fail to win against the Saints, they will have made footballing history by winning the league championship ten times in a row.

The Gers have the marginally easier fixture. Celtic's opponents, St Johnstone, need to beat Celtic to be in with a chance of claiming fourth place and a UEFA cup spot.

Kilmarnock, the present fourth place team know that they must win to ensure they hold onto the place. Their opponents, Hibs, would probably have presented more of a threat, but the previous week, having failed to win against Dundee United, they were relegated.

Hearts facing Dunfermline have nothing to play for, having secured third place weeks earlier. They know they will be playing in Europe no matter what. But the players are keen to put themselves in Jim Jefferies' thoughts when it comes to Cup Final team selections. This ensures, for the fans at least, that the game will be entertaining.

The most meaningless match lies between Motherwell and Aberdeen at Fir Park. If it wasn't for next season's league reconstruction this could have been a relegation playoff decider.

The only certainty on this most exciting of days is that there will be an inordinate amount of ears tuned to radios throughout all of Scotland's grounds.

THE TEAMS	STARTING LINE UP	WHAT'S AT STAKE...
CELTIC v **ST JOHNSTONE**	Gould, Boyd, Annoni, McNamara, Rieper, Stubbs, Larsson, Burley, Donnelly, Lambert, O'Donnell	**THE TITLE**
	Main, McQuillan, Preston, Sekerlioglu, McCluskey, Whiteford, O'Halloran, O'Neill, Grant, O'Boyle, Jenkinson	**EUROPEAN PLACE**
DUNDEE UNITED v **RANGERS**	Dykstra, Jenkins, Malpas, Skoldmark, Jonsson, Bowman, Olafsson, Zetterlund, McSwegan, Easton, McLaren	**NOTHING**
	Niemi, Porrini, Stensaas, Gough, Amoruso, Bjorklund, Gattuso, Ferguson, Durie I, Albertz, Laudrup	**THE TITLE**
HEARTS v **DUNFERMLINE**	Rousset, McPherson, Naysmith, Weir, McManus, Flogel, McCann, Fulton, Robertson, Adam, Quitongo	**NOTHING**
	Westwater, Shields, McCulloch, Tod, Ireland, Huxford, Britton, Squires, Smith, Bingham, Millar M	**NOTHING**
KILMARNOCK v **HIBERNIAN**	Marshall, McPherson, Kerr, Lauchlan, Montgomerie, Burke, Reilly, Nevin, Holt, Roberts, Vareille	**EUROPEAN PLACE**
	Gunn, Miller W, Elliott, Renwick, Hughes, Dods, Tosh, Miller K, Crawford, Laverty, McGinlay	**NOTHING**
MOTHERWELL v **ABERDEEN**	Thompson, May, McMillan, Denham, Martin, Ross, Valikarri, Shivute, Coyne, Davies, Coyle, McCulloch (s), Craigan (s), Sullivan (s)	**NOTHING**
	Leighton, Anderson, Whyte, Buchan, Inglis, Smith, Young, Jess, Newell, Dodds, Gillies, O'Neil, B (s), Rowson (s), Wyness (s)	**NOTHING**

Allsport

The last day of the season

THE TEAMS	🕐 5 MINS PLAYED	🕐 10 MINS PLAYED	🕐 15 MINS PLAYED
CELTIC v **ST JOHNSTONE**	**Larsson** settles the Bhoys' nerves, sweeping a 25-yard left-foot drive past Alan Main. The fans begin celebrating. The championship is clearly in sight. **Gooaall!**	Looking to have cast off all of their doubts, Celtic settle into a confident style of play. A penalty claim is turned down by Hugh Dallas.	Celtic are all over St Johnstone. Not content with a single goal, Celtic put on a power performance in search of that second goal which will kill off hope for the Saints.
DUNDEE UNITED v **RANGERS**	A tense start is disrupted with the news from Celtic Park of Henrik Larsson's strike. 30,00 fans remain at Ibrox watching on the big screen.	With the helicopter waiting to take team and manager to Ibrox with the trophy, Rangers are doing most of the attacking, although United are not giving it up easily.	Rangers are all over United with the news from Celtic Park ringing in the ears of both teams.
HEARTS v **DUNFERMLINE**	Dunfermline start the game in fighting mood. A hooked shot from **Andy Smith** is cleared off the line from **Davie Weir**. Two minutes later **Gilles Rousset** saves well from a close range **Gerry Britton** shot.	**Neil McCann** isn't quite able to work his magic on a robust looking Dunfermline. **Alan McManus** is notable in the Hearts defence.	**Neil McCann** is instrumental in the regaining of the midfield for Hearts. He forces a good save from **Ian Westwater** after **John Robertson** had put him clear.
KILMARNOCK v **HIBERNIAN**	Killie field the team that beat Rangers at Ibrox the previous week. Killie fans watch celebration as Celtic go ahead at Celtic Park. Radios become superglued to ears.	Hibs play at magnificent pace, putting the home defence under severe pressure. The pressure is absorbed and Kilmarnock begin making chances for themselves.	Kilmarnock put themselves into the European driving seat with a well worked goal supplied from **Pat Nevin** for **Mark Roberts**. **Gooaall!**
MOTHERWELL v **ABERDEEN**	90 seconds on the watch and **McMillian** clears the ball in the Wells' box with his hand. Aberdeen's **Billy Dodds** steps up to take the penalty and scores. **Gooaall!**	The Well regroup and fight off further Dons challenges, the early strike gives some hope that this won't be an insignificant kick-about.	A summer Saturday, with holidays and France 98 in the distance, seems more on the minds of players and fans. **zzZZZZZ!**

⏱ 20 MINS PLAYED	⏱ 25 MINS PLAYED	⏱ 30 MINS PLAYED
Pushing all men forward but the goalkeeper, St Johnstone's box begins to resemble the last stand at the Alamo. Surely they can't hold out any longer?	**Larsson** lobs **Alan Main** who is off his goal. It doesn't go in. Celtic deserve to add another. They look like they're going to cruise this match.	The fans get restless. **Brian Laudrup** has scored for Rangers at Tannadice. St Johnstone's box resembles a pinball table with the ball pinging off everyone.
Rangers' play becomes scrappy, whether it's external pressure or the 'other game' is open to question. **zzzzzzzz!**	Following a 25-yard drive from Rangers' **Bowman** that is forced over by **Nemi**, former Rangers' player **Gary McSwegan** takes a pass by **Craig Easton** and skies the chance.	**Amoruso** sends **Laudrup** through a square United defence, the Dane slots the ball in the bottom corner. Fans at Tannadice and Ibrox go wild. **Gooaall!**
It's end-to-end stuff as Hearts begin to put on a show. Dunfermline hit the post. Hearts break out of their own box and show their clinical efficiency when **Adam** fires them into the lead. **Gooaall!**	**Davie Weir** slips through a perfect ball for **Stephane Adam** to break clear. He makes no mistake and cracks home a beautiful opener. **Gooaall!**	End-to-end stuff encourages the Hearts fans for the upcoming Cup Final against Rangers.
Kilmarnock begin to look like a team who deserve to be playing in Europe. **Gary Holt** just fails to keep control of the ball when he is one-on-one with the keeper.	**Stevie Crawford** in a rare Hibs attack fires a ball over the bar. Hibs look as if they want to go down fighting.	**Mark Reilly**, captain for the day, is taken off for treatment to a face injury. When he doesn't return after five minutes, **Ali Mitchell** is sent on to replace him.
Billy Dodds seems to be taking the game seriously as, in the 22nd minute, he takes a pass from **Mike Newell** dummy's keeper **Thompson** and slams the ball home. 2-0. **Gooaall!**	**Mike Newell**, a hero just minutes earlier, turns villain as he squanders a 10-yard chance from a sweet **Eion Jess** ball.	With nothing to play for but pride, and even that in mediocre rags, neither side seem to want to commit to anything other than clumsy challenges and missed passes.

> "We will be going to Parkhead to win because we have to if we are to have a chance of a European place."
> – Paul Sturrock, St Johnstone's manager

> "Everybody knows it's been a poor season for us and work is under way already to improve things."
> – Paul Hegarty, Aberdeen's assistant manager

> "I'd far rather be in Celtic's position. They are totally in the driving seat."
> – Ally McCoist

Allsport

The last day of the season

THE TEAMS	🕐 35 MINS PLAYED	🕐 40 MINS PLAYED	🕐 45 MINS PLAYED
CELTIC **v** **ST JOHNSTONE**	Celtic set up camp in St Johnstone's half. **Boyd** fails to set up **Burley** for a shot. Their urgency can only result in that elusive championship goal.	St Johnstone's confidence is growing. They sense from the reaction of the fans that Rangers must be in the lead. They continue to press and begin to look like the team most likely to score.	A tense end to the first half.
DUNDEE UNITED **v** **RANGERS**	Not to be outdone by Laudrup, **Gordon Durie** bears down on the Terrors' goal only to send his chip wide of former QPR keeper **Dykstra**'s goal.	Rangers look unconvincing until **Albertz** slots a great ball through to full-back **Stensaas** who sees his shot blocked by **Dykstra**.	Hero **Amoruso** is booked for a foul on **Gary McSwegan** as half-time bears down on the Blue-side of Glasgow. Walter Smith must look to make changes.
HEARTS **v** **DUNFERMLINE**	**McPherson** combining well with **Quitongo** almost snatch another with overlapping runs and clever interchanges.	**Gary Naysmith** comes close to grabbing a cheeky second. Breaking free on the left flank he forces **Westwater** into conceding a corner.	The final five minutes are played through with Hearts looking increasingly threatening.
KILMARNOCK **v** **HIBERNIAN**	**Dylan Kerr** just fails to add to Kilmarnock's lead when a free kick rises over the bar.	The Edinburgh samba band get ready for the first-half celebrations which ensure a carnival atmosphere at Rugby Park.	Killie's fans become even happier after hearing on the radio that Partick Thistle have equalised against local rivals Ayr. Ayr can be relegated if Partick win today.
MOTHERWELL **v** **ABERDEEN**	The game goes on with the ball floating around in midfield and the fans waiting for history to unfold elsewhere. zzZZZZZZ!	The game settles down to a to-and-fro exchange of passes and giveaways with no one committing and no one seemingly that interested in the result.	Motherwell seem to have nothing to offer in return two **Dodds**' two strikes. Are the players thinking about holidays?

Allsport

🕐 50 MINS PLAYED	🕐 55 MINS PLAYED	🕐 60 MINS PLAYED
		Rieper clears off the line. The muteness of the fans begins to pick up as they try to get behind their team. **Harald Brattbakk** comes on for Donnelly as Celtic push, pull and push again for the killer goal.
Immediate pressure from Celtic in the second half. **Larsson** gets needlessly caught offside and St Johnstone go hunting.	**Gould** just clears a dodgy passback from the Celtic defence. **Main** saves from a **Donnelly** effort which should have gone into the net.	
Stuart McCall comes on for Joachim Bkorkland and wins a penalty. A furious **Maurice Malpas** is booked for picking up the ball, but **Albertz** strikes the ball home. Go**oaall!**	Still two up and rampant by now, all Celtic have to do is concede one and the history could be made.	The Terrors aren't prepared to play a bit-part as **Zetterland** flicks a header into the Rangers' net. Walter Smith responds as **McCoist** comes on from Laudrup. Go**oaall!**
Hearts defence, so assured in the first half, becomes increasingly shaky as Dunfermline's half-time team talk seems to have hit its mark.	**Steve Fulton** gifts a ball to **Andy Tod** who comes within inches of levelling the score.	**Rousset** sends a clearance to **Gerry Britton** The Dunfermline striker immediately has a crack at goal which Rousset has to dive well to save.
The Killie fans begin chanting the name of their favourite manager as **Gordon Marshall** makes his first save of the match from a shot by **Barry Laverty**.	Contentness flits through Killie's play. **Pat McGinlay** is booked when he pulls down **Pat Nevin** on the wing. Nevin had broken clear and was threatening the Hibs goal.	The tempo of the match slows down. Each side look content for the flow of the play to continue as it has been going on. zz**zZZZZ!**
The games continues with no visible sign that anyone will commit one way or another. zz**zZZZZ!**	With the news from elsewhere courting all the interest, the play on Fir Park takes on the appearance of a Sunday kick-about.	Nothing... nothing but the sound of radios crackling the news from Glasgow and Dundee.

Allsport

After Larsson's first Celtic goal inside of five minutes, the Bhoys are all over St Johnstone with a power performance that's looking for a second goal.

The Saints' John McQuinlan makes a brave effort, but a sliding tackle from O'Donnell stops it short.

The last day of the season

THE TEAMS	🕐 65 MINS PLAYED	🕐 70 MINS PLAYED	🕐 75 MINS PLAYED
CELTIC v **ST JOHNSTONE**	**Gerry McMahon** comes on for Keith O'Halloran to try and open up the options in the right-hand side of the park. **Rieper**'s head once again saves Celtic from conceding a championship losing goal.	The crowd have kittens as St Johnstone begin to become more menacing with their threat.	**Brattbakk** breaks the tension with the goal that transforms him into an immortal. Breaking into the box, he scores a delightful goal after he picks up a beautifully-flighted cross from **Jackie McNamara**. Go**oaall!**
DUNDEE UNITED v **RANGERS**	The change of **McCoist** for Laudrup enables Rangers to regroup and attempt to consolidate their lead.	Laudrup's speed is missing as **McCoist** tries to get used to the pace of the game. zz**zzzZZ!**	The news of Brattbakks' goal from Celtic Park begins to filter through. The United fans start goading Rangers with chants of "Championes!" mimicking the cries from Celtic Park.
HEARTS v **DUNFERMLINE**	**Steve Fulton** shows some intelligent passing as he combines with **Weir** and **McPherson** in setting up clever counter attacks.	**Andy Smith** threatens the Hearts goal but is cancelled out by the alertness of **Dave McPherson**.	**Lee Makel**'s replacement for **McCann** looks as if it's been a good move. His clever movement on and off the ball ensures that McCann is not missed.
KILMARNOCK v **HIBERNIAN**	The game keeps up the tussling in the midfield. **Pat Nevin** looks threatening every time he manages to get on the ball.	**Jerome Vareille** begins to look tired. His continuous running at the Hibs defence looks as if it may get a result.	Killies fans celebrate Celtic's second goal as they realise that nothing can stop them from reaching Europe in a second consecutive season. Hibs look increasingly likely to score an equaliser.
MOTHERWELL v **ABERDEEN**	At last, a combination of passes from Motherwell's **Tommy Coyne** and **Owen Coyle** put midfielder **Ian Ross** through on goal. Ross finishes coolly. Go**oaall!**	With the game snorring into even more insignificance, **McMillian** scores to for the Well to make a game of it.	The three points which look very much in the Dons' pockets will be enough to raise them to sixth place.

⏱ 80 MINS PLAYED	⏱ 85 MINS PLAYED	⏱ 90 MINS PLAYED
A double substitution from St Johnstone in an attempt to inject some freshness into tired legs looks like the last throw of the die from manager Paul Sturrock.	Celtic's reserve players begin gathering in the Celtic tunnel. They are as eager to join in the celebrations as everyone else.	Brattbakk **almost adds another goal.** **Blinker** finally comes on as a substitute to savour the fantastic atmosphere.
It's going from bad to worse as the atmosphere gets to goal-maker **Albertz** and he is sent off for violent conduct.	You can almost hear the Celtic fans calling as the game and the championship heads into its dying minutes.	It's all down to Celtic now as whatever Rangers or Dundee United do will not affect the big picture.
Derek Holmes slips past a competent Dunfermline defence to slide the ball away from **Ian Westwater**. The goal surely increases his chances of Cup duty. **Gooaall!**	Hearts look content to settle for a two-goal victory. Dunfermline at this point look as if they have run out of ideas. **zzzzZZZZ!**	Hearts play out the game to celebrate their last league victory of the season. Jim Jefferies will have no problem in making his selection for their cup game.
"Come on you Hibees" is the dominant chant as Hibernian take the ascendancy. Killie don't seem to care. They're going to Europe no matter what.	Hibs look as if they have missed the presence of young **Grant Brebner**. His assurance could have altered the balance of play in the midfield.	**Stevie Crawford** scores for the Hibees. Due to the result in Glasgow, no one cares. Most minds are already thinking about the pitch invasion. **Gooaall!**
The game is buried now beneath the news from Tannadice and Celtic Park, transitor radios are more to the fore than scarves or quality passing.	Both teams seem to be looking at the clock now, more and more voices in the crowd are raised in discussion of events elsewhere.	**Jim Leighton,** with an eye to France 98, retains his concentration to pull off an awesome close-range save from Well's **Coyne.**

> **"It's been a great season, we've done well and we'll play in Europe."**
> – Pat Nevin

> **"I'd like to congratulate Celtic football club, I know how hard it is to win a championship."** – Richard Gough

> **"We deserved to win it and we done it."**
> – Paul Lambert

Harald Brattbakk puts the ball past Alan Main for Celtic's second goal – and really, it's all over...

It's all over
Premiership 1997-98

Celtic finally broke the dominance of Rangers with a show of skill and nerve in the final league match. This was how the unfolding drama of the last ever Scottish Premier League finished up.

	P	W	D	L	F	A	Pts
Celtic	36	22	8	6	64	24	74
Rangers	36	21	9	6	76	38	72
Hearts	36	18	10	7	70	46	67
Kilmarnock	36	13	11	12	40	52	50
St Johnstone	36	13	10	13	38	42	48
Aberdeen	36	9	12	15	39	53	39
Dundee United	36	8	13	15	43	51	37
Dunfermline	36	8	13	15	43	68	37
Motherwell	36	9	7	20	46	64	34
Hibernian	36	6	12	18	37	58	30

Lowest Attendance:
St Johnstone v Kilmarnock
4,385 – 13th December

Highest Attendance:
Celtic v Saint Johnstone
50,140 – 9th May

Fastest Goal:
O'Neill, 58 seconds, Saint Johnstone
v Kilmarnock, 28th March

Biggest Victory:
Rangers 7 Dunfermline 0
18th October

Highest Aggregate:
8 Motherwell 6 Hibernian 2
31st January

HIGHEST SCORERS

Aberdeen	Billy Dodds	10
Celtic	Henrick Larsson	16
Dundee United	Kjell Olofsson	19
Dunfermline	Andy Smith	16
Hearts	Jim Hamilton	14
Hibernian	Steve Crawford	9
Kilmarnock	Paul Wright	10
Motherwell	Tommy Coyne	14
Rangers	Marco Negri	32
St Johnstone	George O'Boyle	10

Photo News Scotland

Photo News Scotland

PREMIERSHIP WINNERS